Thurber Country

A New Collection of Pieces
About Males and Females,
Mainly of Our
Own Species,

by

JAMES THURBER

SIMON AND SCHUSTER: NEW YORK

FIFTH PAPERBACK PRINTING, 1963

Of the 25 pieces included in this book, the following appeared originally in *The New Yorker*: "The Figgerin' of Aunt Wilma," "The White Rabbit Caper," "What a Lovely Generalization!" "The Interview," "File and Forget," "Do You Want to Make Something Out of It?" "The Case of Dimity Ann," "A Final Note on Chanda Bell," "There's a Time for Flags," "A Friend of the Earth," "The American Literary Scene," "Teacher's Pet," "Shake Hands with Birdey Doggett," "*What* Cocktail Party?" and "*Joyeux Noël*, Mr. Dunning.

"My Own Ten Rules for a Happy Marriage" appeared originally in *Cosmopolitan* Magazine.

"The Girls in the Closet," and "The Pleasure Cruise and How to Survive It" appeared originally in *Holiday* Magazine.

All of the other pieces appeared originally in *The Bermudian*, and their inclusion in this volume represents their first publication in this country.

LIBRARY OF CONGRESS CATALOG
CARD NUMBER: 53-9700
DEWEY DECIMAL CLASSIFICATION
NUMBER: 817
MANUFACTURED IN THE UNITED STATES OF AMERICA

Most of the pieces in this book originally appeared in *The New Yorker*. The rest of them, in somewhat different form, were printed in other magazines: seven in *The Bermudian*, two in *Holiday*, and one in *Cosmopolitan*.

Contents

1. What's So Funny?   1
2. The Figgerin' of Aunt Wilma   9
3. The White Rabbit Caper   23
4. Back Home Again   35
5. My Own Ten Rules for a Happy Marriage   41
6. What a Lovely Generalization!   52
7. The Interview   58
8. Lady in a Trap   75
9. File and Forget   83
10. The Case Book of James Thurber   100
11. The Case of Dimity Ann   106
12. Look at That Darling Thing!   121
13. Do You Want to Make Something Out of It?   127
14. Take Her Up Tenderly   138
15. The Girls in the Closet   143
16. A Final Note on Chanda Bell   151
17. There's a Time for Flags   165
18. A Friend of the Earth   177
19. The American Literary Scene   189
20. Teacher's Pet   199
21. Shake Hands with Birdey Doggett   213
22. *What* Cocktail Party?   219
23. *Joyeux Noël*, Mr. Durning   231
24. See No Weevil   253
25. The Pleasure Cruise, and How to Survive It   260

CHAPTER ONE

What's So Funny?

A YOUNG LADY, Miss E. H., of Oklahoma City, has written me asking if there are any standing rules for writing humor. I am naturally flattered to have been selected as an official spokesman in this matter, and I hope I will not intone as I go along, or become too pontifical, or turn surly.

Perhaps we might begin with a caption for a drawing I have had around for years: "Where were you all night, Chastity?" This is known to the trade as a Formula Caption, or one that is subject to endless variations: "Quit messing around with that loaded pistol, Prudence," and "For Heaven's sake, Patience, will you please give me a chance to explain?" There are many formula situations with which every magazine reader is familiar: the man falling from a building and saying something to a girl in an office on his way down; the man and the girl cast away on a raft in the ocean; the two artisans working on the face of a gigantic clock; and the two beachcombers on the beach discussing what they have come there to forget. This last, by the way, was best done nearly forty years ago in what must have been its original version: the First Beachcomber says, "What did you come here to forget?" and the Second Beachcomber says, "I've forgotten." So much for formulas in comic art.

I have established a few standing rules of my own about humor, after receiving dozens of humorous essays and stories from strangers over a period of twenty years. 1) The reader should be able to find out what the story is about. 2) Some inkling of the general idea should be apparent in the first five hundred words. 3) If the writer has decided to change the name of his protagonist from Ketcham to McTavish, Ketcham should not keep bobbing up in the last five pages. A good way to eliminate this confusion is to read the piece over before sending it out, and remove Ketcham completely. He is a nuisance. 4) The word "I'll" should not be divided so that the "I" is on one line and " 'll" on the next. The reader's attention, after the breaking up of "I'll," can never be successfully recaptured. 5) It also never recovers from such names as Ann S. Thetic, Maud Lynn, Sally Forth, Bertha Twins, and the like. 6) Avoid comic stories about plumbers who are mistaken for surgeons, sheriffs who are terrified by gunfire, psychiatrists who are driven crazy by women patients, doctors who faint at the sight of blood, adolescent girls who know more about sex than their fathers do, and midgets who turn out to be the parents of a two-hundred-pound wrestler.

I have a special wariness of people who write opening sentences with nothing in mind, and then try to create a story around them. These sentences, usually easy to detect, go like this: "Mrs. Ponsonby had never put the dog in the oven before," " 'I have a wine tree, if you would care to see it,' said Mr. Dillingworth," and "Jackson decided suddenly, for no reason, really, to buy his wife a tricycle." I have never traced the fortunes of such characters in the stories I receive beyond the opening sentence, but, like you, I have a fair notion of what happens, or doesn't happen, in "The Barking Oven," "The Burgundy Tree," and "A Tricycle for Mama."

An aging author who receives, but never has the time or strength to read, humorous stories written by women that invariably run to 8,500 words, can usually get a pretty good idea of the material from the accompanying letters, many of which contain snapshots of the writer's husband, baby, and beach cottage. These pieces have usually been written in a gay, carefree vacation mood, and it is a sound rule to avoid self-expression at such a time, since it leads to overemphasis, underlining, unnecessary quotation marks, and the odd notion that everything that happens is funny. The American housewife, possibly as the result of what might be called the "Blandings Influence," also seems to believe that amusement is inherent in everything that goes wrong about the house and in everybody that comes in to fix it. My own experience has not been that fortunate. In my view, a carpenter named Twippley is likely to be as dull as a professor named Tweedle, and I think we are safe in setting this up as a standing rule.

Another reliable rule, Miss E. H., is that nocturnal urges to get out of bed and write something humorous should be strongly resisted. The woman who springs up, lights the light, wakes her husband, and starts "writing it out" is not only a nuisance, but is almost certainly laboring under the common illusion of the sleepy that the commonplace is remarkable. These night pieces are usually dashed off in less than twenty minutes, and when written by the female, seem to grow out of the conviction that writing late at night lends a special magic to prose, like writing in a rose arbor or on a houseboat. The magic, alas, rarely survives the cynical light of day. Tender is the night, but it has neither literary style nor creative talent, and no more enhances the quality of a lady's output than does the assumption of such cute and booksy *noms de plume* as Suzanna Prynne or Priscilla Winkle.

What's So Funny?

SINCE I WAS twelve, I have had an antipathy to ladies or gentlemen who write comic stories in baby talk, Deep Southern dialect, or other exasperating lingos, or whose characters lisp, or stammer, or talk like Red Skelton. I am also distinctly cool to writers who try to interest me in tribal dialect, African, Mayan, or American Indian. My worst personal experience in that field was when I read, or tried to read, a manuscript dealing with the confused whimsies of the Shoshone Indians. Its author sent a letter with it that began: "I have lived among the Shoshones for twenty years, and have thought for some time that their humor, which consists mainly of heavy banter, would be a valuable contribution to American folklore. In some instances, as in the case of OGLA WAHGU, which is not easily rendered into English, I have made no attempt at translation. OGLA WAHGU means, variously, 'not for me,' and 'I am going,' and, more rarely, 'strook him.' " My secretary returned the manuscript with a polite letter saying that I had died.

There ought to be a law, Miss E. H., and not merely a rule, against the sort of thing that emerges when an authoress—she is usually either very young or in her treacherous fifties—"invents" what she calls a new kind of humor. This stuff, out of "Tender Buttons" by "Jabberwocky," is even less clear than the kidding around of the Shoshones. One example began: "He was in bad, but she knew he was not a sloop." Another

5

What's So Funny?

"Private Lives," Miss E. H., signed with the name "Knowall Coward," I will burn the snapshot of you and your husband and the beach cottage. As for your poor baby—but I am getting surly now and will close, with best wishes, love and kisses, and a friendly warning that humor can be a headache, dear Miss E. H. Why don't you become a bacteriologist, or a Red Cross nurse, or a Wave, like all the other girls?

                                        Cordially yours.

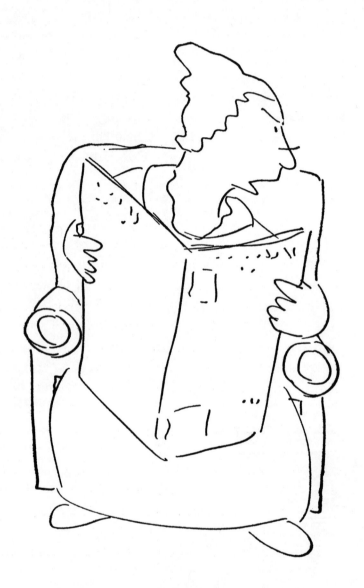

CHAPTER TWO

The Figgerin' of Aunt Wilma

WHEN I WAS a boy, John Hance's grocery stood on the south side of Town Street, just east of Fourth, in the Central Market region of Columbus, Ohio. It was an old store even then, forty-five years ago, and its wide oak floor boards had been worn pleasantly smooth by the shoe soles of three generations of customers. The place smelled of coffee, peppermint, vinegar, and spices. Just inside the door on the left, a counter with a rounded glass front held all the old-fashioned penny candies—gumdrops, licorice whips, horehound, and the rest—some of them a little pale with age. On the rear wall, between a barrel of dill pickles and a keg of salt mackerel in brine, there was an iron coffee grinder, whose handle I was sometimes allowed to turn.

Once, Mr. Hance gave me a stick of Yucatan gum,

an astonishing act of generosity, since he had a sharp
sense of the value of a penny. Thrift was John Hance's
religion. His store was run on a strictly cash basis. He
shared the cost of his telephone with the Hays Carriage Shop, next door. The instrument was set in a
movable wooden cubicle that could be whirled
through an opening in the west wall of the store. When
I was ten, I used to hang around the grocery on Saturday afternoons, waiting for the telephone to disappear into the wall. Then I would wait for it to swing
back again. It was a kind of magic, and I was disappointed to learn of its mundane purpose—the saving
of a few dollars a month.

Mr. Hance was nearly seventy, a short man with
white hair and a white mustache and the most alert
eyes that I can remember, except perhaps Aunt Wilma
Hudson's. Aunt Wilma lived on South Sixth Street
and always shopped at Mr. Hance's store. Mr.
Hance's eyes were blue and capable of a keen con-
centration that could make you squirm. Aunt Wilma
had black agate eyes that moved restlessly and scrutinized everybody with bright suspicion. In church,
her glance would dart around the congregation seeking out irreverent men and women whose expressions
showed that they were occupied with worldly concerns, or even carnal thoughts, in the holy place. If
she lighted on a culprit, her heavy, dark brows would
lower, and her mouth would tighten in righteous dis-

The Figgerin' of Aunt Wilma

approval. Aunt Wilma was as honest as the day is long and as easily confused, when it came to what she called figgerin', as the night is dark. Her clashes with Mr. Hance had become a family legend. He was a swift and competent calculator, and nearly fifty years of constant practice had enabled him to add up a column of figures almost at a glance. He set down his columns swiftly on an empty paper sack with a stubby black pencil. Aunt Wilma, on the other hand, was slow and painstaking when it came to figgerin'. She would go over and over a column of numbers, her glasses far down on her nose, her lips moving soundlessly. To her, rapid calculation, like all the other reckless and impulsive habits of men, was tainted with a kind of godlessness. Mr. Hance always sighed when he looked up and saw her coming into his store. He knew that she could lift a simple dollar transaction into a dim and mystic realm of confusion all her own.

I WAS FORTUNATE enough to be present one day in 1905 when Mr. Hance's calculating and Aunt Wilma's figgerin' came together in memorable single combat. She had wheedled me into carrying her market basket, on the ground that it was going to be too heavy for her to manage. Her two grandsons, boys around my own age, had skipped out when I came to call at their house, and Aunt Wilma promptly seized on me. A young'un, as she called everybody under seventeen, was not worth his salt if he couldn't help a body about the house. I had shopped with her before, under duress, and I knew her accustomed and invariable route on Saturday mornings, when Fourth Street, from Main to State, was lined with the stands of truck gardeners. Prices were incredibly low in those days, but Aunt Wilma questioned the cost, the quality, and the measure of everything. By the time she had finished her long and tedious purchases of fresh produce from the country, and we had turned east into Town Street and headed for Mr. Hance's store, the weight of the market basket was beginning to pain my arm. "Come along, child, come along," Aunt Wilma snapped, her eyes shining with the look of the Middle Western housewife engaged in hard but virtuous battle with the wicked forces of the merchandising world.

I saw Mr. Hance make a small involuntary gesture with his right hand as he spied Aunt Wilma coming through the door. He had just finished with a customer, and since his assistant was busy, he knew he was in for it. It took a good half hour for Aunt Wilma to complete her shopping for groceries, but at length everything she wanted was stacked on the counter in sacks and cans and boxes. Mr. Hance set deftly to work with his paper sack and pencil, jotting down the price of each article as he fitted it into the basket. Aunt Wilma watched his expert movements closely,

The Figgerin' of Aunt Wilma

like a hostile baseball fan waiting for an error in the infield. She regarded adroitness in a man as "slick" rather than skillful.

Aunt Wilma's purchases amounted to ninety-eight cents. After writing down this sum, Mr. Hance, knowing my aunt, whisked the paper bag around on the counter so that she could examine his addition. It took her some time, bending over and peering through her glasses, to arrive at a faintly reluctant corroboration of his figgerin'. Even when she was satisfied that all was in order, she had another go at the column of numbers, her lips moving silently as she added them up for the third time. Mr. Hance waited patiently, the flat of his hands on the counter. He seemed to be fascinated by the movement of her lips. "Well, I guess it's all right," said Aunt Wilma, at last, "but everything *is* so dear." What she had bought for less than a dollar made the market basket bulge. Aunt Wilma took her purse out of her bag and drew out a dollar bill slowly and handed it over, as if it were a hundred dollars she would never see again.

Mr. Hance deftly pushed the proper keys of the cash register, and the red hand on the indicator pointed to $.98. He studied the cash drawer, which had shot out at him. "Well, well," he said, and then, "Hmm. Looks like I haven't got any pennies." He turned back to Aunt Wilma. "Have you got three cents, Mrs. Hudson?" he asked.

13

That started it.

Aunt Wilma gave him a quick look of distrust. Her Sunday suspicion gleamed in her eyes. "*You* owe *me* *two* cents," she said sharply.

"I know that, Mrs. Hudson," he sighed, "but I'm out of pennies. Now, if you'll give me three cents, I'll give you a nickel."

Aunt Wilma stared at him cautiously.

"It's all right if you give him three cents and he gives you a nickel," I said.

"Hush up," said Aunt Wilma. "I'm figgerin'." She figgered for several moments, her mouth working again.

Mr. Hance slipped a nickel out of the drawer and placed it on the counter. "There is your nickel," he said firmly. "Now you just have to give me three cents."

Aunt Wilma pecked about in her purse and located three pennies, which she brought out carefully, one at a time. She laid them on the counter beside the nickel, and Mr. Hance reached for them. Aunt Wilma was too quick for him. She covered the eight cents with a lean hand. "Wait, now!" she said, and she took her hand away slowly. She frowned over the four coins as if they were a difficult hand in bridge whist. She ran her lower lip against her upper teeth. "Maybe if I give you a dime," she said, "and take the eight cents . . . It is *two* cents you're short, ain't it?"

14

The Figgerin' of Aunt Wilma

Mr. Hance began to show signs of agitation. One or two amused customers were now taking in the scene out of the corners of their eyes. "No, no," said Mr. Hance. "That way, you would be making me a present of seven cents!" This was too much for Aunt Wilma. She couldn't understand the new and preposterous sum of seven cents that had suddenly leaped at her from nowhere. The notion that she was about to do herself out of some money staggered her, and her eyes glazed for a moment like a groggy prizefighter's. Neither Mr. Hance nor I said anything, out of fear of deepening the tangle. She made an uncertain move of her right hand and I had the wild thought that she was going to give Mr. Hance one of the pennies and scoop up the seven cents, but she didn't. She fell into a silent clinch with the situation and then her eyes cleared. "Why, of *course*!" she cried brightly. "I don't know what got into me! You take the eight cents and give me a dime. Then I'll have the two cents that's coming to me." One of the customers laughed, and Aunt Wilma cut him down with a swift glare. The diversion gave me time to figure out that whereas Mr. Hance had been about to gain seven cents, he was now going to lose a nickel. "That way, *I* would be making *you* a present of *five* cents, Mrs. Hudson," he said stiffly. They stood motionless for several seconds, each trying to stare the other down.

"Now, here," said Mr. Hance, turning and taking

her dollar out of the still open cash drawer. He laid it beside the nickel and the pennies. "Now, here," he said again. "You gave me a dollar three, but you don't owe me a dollar three—you owe me five cents less than that. Here is the five cents." He snatched it up and handed it to her. She held the nickel between thumb and forefinger, and her eyes gleamed briefly, as if she at last comprehended the peculiar deal, but the gleam faded. Suddenly she handed him his nickel and picked up her dollar and her three cents. She put the pennies back in her purse. "I've rung up the ninety-eight cents, Mrs. Hudson," said Mr. Hance quickly. "I must put the dollar back in the till." He turned and pointed at the $.98 on the indicator. "I tell you what. If you'll give me the dollar, I'll give you the nickel and we'll call it square." She obviously didn't want to take the nickel or give up the dollar, but she did, finally. I was astounded at first, for here was the penny-careful Mr. Hance knocking three cents off a bill, but then I realized he was afraid of losing the dollar and was willing to settle for the lesser of two evils.

"Well," said Aunt Wilma irritably, "I'm sure I don't know what you're trying to do."

I was a timid boy, but I had to plunge into the snarl, if only on behalf of the family honor. "Gee, Aunt Wilma," I told her, "if you keep the nickel, he's giving you everything for ninety-five cents."

Mr. Hance scowled hard at me. He was afraid I

was going to get him in deeper than he already was. "It's all right, son," he said. "It's all right." He put the dollar in the till and shoved the drawer shut with a decisive bang, but I wasn't going to give up.

"Gee whizz, Aunt Wilma," I complained, "you still owe him three cents. Don't you see that?"

She gave me the pitying glance of a superior and tired intelligence. "I never owed him three cents in my life," she said tartly. "He owes me two cents. You stay out of things you don't understand."

"It's all right," said Mr. Hance again, in a weary voice. He was sure that if she scrabbled in her purse again for the three pennies, she would want her dollar back, and they would be right where they had started. I gave my aunt a look of disenchantment.

"Now, wait!" she cried suddenly. "Maybe I have the exact change! I don't know what's got into me I didn't think of that! I think I have the right change after all." She put back on the counter the nickel she had been clutching in her left hand, and then she began to peck at the coins in her purse and, after a good minute, arranged two quarters, four dimes, Mr. Hance's nickel, and three pennies on the counter. "There," she said, her eyes flashing triumph. "Now you give me my dollar back."

Mr. Hance sighed deeply, rang out the cash drawer by pushing "No Sale," and handed her the dollar. Then he hastily scraped up the change, deposited each coin in its proper place in the till, and slammed the drawer shut again. I was only ten, and mathematics was not my best study, but it wasn't hard to figure that Mr. Hance, who in the previous arrangement had been out three cents, was now out five cents. "Good day, Mrs. Hudson," he said grimly. He felt my sympathetic eyes on him, and we exchanged a brief, knowing masculine glance of private understanding.

"Good day, Mr. Hance," said Aunt Wilma, and her tone was as grim as the grocer's.

I took the basket from the counter, and Mr. Hance sighed again, this time with relief. "Goodbye, goodbye," he said with false heartiness, glad to see us on our way. I felt I should slip him the parsley, or whatever sack in the basket had cost a nickel.

"Come on, child," said Aunt Wilma. "It's dreadfully late. I declare it's taken hours to shop today." She muttered plaintively all the way out of the store.

I noticed as I closed the door behind us that Mr. Hance was waiting on a man customer. The man was laughing. Mr. Hance frowned and shrugged.

As WE WALKED east on Town Street, Aunt Wilma let herself go. "I never heard of such a thing in all the born days of my life," she said. "I don't know where John Hance got his schooling, if he got any. The very idea—a grown man like that getting so mixed up. Why, I could have spent the whole day in that store

The Figgerin' of Aunt Wilma

and he'd never of figgered it out. Let him keep the two cents, then. It was worth it to get out of that store."

"*What* two cents, Aunt Wilma?" I almost squealed.

"Why, the two cents he still owes me!" she said. "I don't know what they teach you young'uns nowadays. Of course he owes me two cents. It come to ninety-eight cents and I give him a dollar. He owed me two cents in the beginning and he still owes me two cents. Your Uncle Herbert will explain it to you. Any man in the world could figger it out except John Hance."

I walked on beside her in silence, thinking of Uncle Herbert, a balding, choleric man of high impatience and quick temper.

"Now, you let *me* explain it to your Uncle Herbert, child," she said. "I declare you were as mixed up as John Hance was. If I'd of listened to you and given him the three cents, like you said, I'd never of got my dollar back. He'd owe me five cents instead of two. Why, it's as plain as day."

I thought I had the solution for her now, and I leaped at it. "That's right, Aunt Wilma," I almost yelled. "He owed you a nickel and he gave you the nickel."

Aunt Wilma stabbed me with her indignation. "I gave *him* the nickel," she said. "I put it on the counter right there under your very eyes, and you saw him scoop it up."

I shifted the market basket to my left arm. "I know,

Aunt Wilma," I said, "but it was *his* nickel all the time."

She snorted. "Well, he's got his precious nickel, ain't he?" she demanded. I shifted the basket again. I thought I detected a faint trace of uneasiness in her tone. She fell silent and quickened her cadence, and it was hard for me to keep up with her. As we turned south into Sixth Street, I glanced up and saw that she was frowning and that her lips were moving again. She was rehearsing the story of the strange transaction for Uncle Herbert. I began to whistle. "Hush up, child," she said. "I'm figgerin'."

UNCLE HERBERT was sitting in the living room, eating an apple. I could tell from his expression that he was in one of his rare amiable moods. Aunt Wilma grabbed the basket away from me. "Now, you let me explain it to your uncle," she said. "You wait till I get back." She sailed out of the room on her way to the kitchen.

A little breathlessly, I told Uncle Herbert the saga of Aunt Wilma's complicated financial quandary. He was chuckling when she came back into the room.

Uncle Herbert's amusement nettled her. "The boy got it wrong," she said accusingly. "He didn't tell it right. He was ever' bit as mixed up as John Hance." Uncle Herbert's chuckle increased to full and open laughter. Aunt Wilma glared at him until he subsided.

The Figgerin' of Aunt Wilma

"Now, Herbert, you listen to me," she began, but he cut in on her.

"If Hance ever gives you that two cents he owes you, Wilma," he said, "I tell you what you have to do to square accounts. Someday you're going to have to give him a dime for three cents." He began to laugh again.

Aunt Wilma Hudson stared at each of us in turn, with a look of fine, cold scorn, and then she raised both her hands and let them fall helplessly. "I declare," she said, "I don't know how the world gets along with the men runnin' it."

CHAPTER THREE

The White Rabbit Caper

(AS THE BOYS WHO TURN OUT THE MYSTERY PROGRAMS ON THE AIR MIGHT WRITE A STORY FOR CHILDREN)

FRED FOX was pouring himself a slug of rye when the door of his office opened and in hopped old Mrs. Rabbit. She was a white rabbit with pink eyes, and she wore a shawl on her head, and gold-rimmed spectacles.

"I want you to find Daphne," she said tearfully, and she handed Fred Fox a snapshot of a white rabbit with pink eyes that looked to him like a picture of every other white rabbit with pink eyes.

"When did she hop the hutch?" asked Fred Fox.

"Yesterday," said old Mrs. Rabbit. "She is only eighteen months old, and I am afraid that some superstitious creature has killed her for one of her feet."

Fred Fox turned the snapshot over and put it in his pocket. "Has this bunny got a throb?" he asked.

"Yes," said old Mrs. Rabbit. "Franz Frog, repulsive owner of the notorious Lily Pad Night Club."

Fred Fox leaped to his feet. "Come on, Grandma," he said, "and don't step on your ears. We got to move fast."

On the way to the Lily Pad Night Club, old Mrs. Rabbit scampered so fast that Fred Fox had all he could do to keep up with her. "Daphne is my great-great-great-great-great-granddaughter, if my memory serves," said old Mrs. Rabbit. "I have thirty-nine thousand descendants."

"This isn't going to be easy," said Fred Fox. "Maybe you should have gone to a magician with a hat."

"But she is the only one named Daphne," said old Mrs. Rabbit, "and she lived alone with me on my great carrot farm."

They came to a broad brook. "Skip it!" said Fred Fox.

"Keep a civil tongue in your head, young man," snapped old Mrs. Rabbit.

Just as they got to the Lily Pad, a dandelion clock struck twelve noon. Fred Fox pushed the button on the great green door, on which was painted a white water lily. The door opened an eighth of an inch, and Ben Rat peered out. "Beat it," he said, but Fred Fox shoved the door open, and old Mrs. Rabbit followed him into a cool green hallway, softly but restlessly

The White Rabbit Caper

lighted by thousands of fireflies imprisoned in the hollow crystal pendants of an enormous chandelier. At
the right there was a flight of green-carpeted stairs,
and at the bottom of the steps the door to the cloakroom. Straight ahead, at the end of the long hallway,
was the cool green door to Franz Frog's office.

"Beat it," said Ben Rat again.

"Talk nice," said Fred Fox, "or I'll seal your house
up with tin. Where's the Croaker?"

"Once a gumpaw, always a gumpaw," grumbled
Ben Rat. "He's in his office."

"With Daphne?"

"Who's Daphne?" asked Ben Rat.

"My great-great-great-great-great-granddaughter," said old Mrs. Rabbit.

"Nobody's that great," snarled Ben Rat.

Fred fox opened the cool green door and went into
Franz Frog's office, followed by old Mrs. Rabbit and
Ben Rat. The owner of the Lily Pad sat behind his
desk, wearing a green suit, green shirt, green tie, green
socks, and green shoes. He had an emerald tiepin and
seven emerald rings. "Whong you wong, Fonnxx?"
he rumbled in a cold, green, cavernous voice. His
eyes bulged and his throat began to swell ominously.

"He's going to croak," explained Ben Rat.

"Nuts," said Fred Fox. "He'll outlive all of us."

"Glunk," croaked Franz Frog.

25

Ben Rat glared at Fred Fox. "You oughta go on the stage," he snarled.

"Where's Daphne?" demanded Fred Fox.

"Hoong Dangneng?" asked Franz Frog.

"Your bunny friend," said Fred Fox.

"Nawng," said Franz Frog.

Fred Fox picked up a cello in a corner and put it down. It was too light to contain a rabbit. The front-door bell rang. "I'll get it," said Fred Fox. It was Oliver (Hoot) Owl, a notorious fly-by-night. "What're you doing up at this hour, Hoot?" asked Fred Fox.

"I'm trying to blind myself, so I'll confess," said Hoot Owl testily.

"Confess to what?" snapped Fred Fox.

"What can't you solve?" asked Hoot Owl.

"The disappearance of Daphne," said Fred Fox.

"Who's Daphne?" asked Hoot Owl.

Franz Frog hopped out of his office into the hall. Ben Rat and old Mrs. Rabbit followed him.

Down the steps from the second floor came Sherman Stork, carrying a white muffler or something and grinning foolishly.

"Well, bless my soul!" said Fred Fox. "If it isn't old mid-husband himself! What did you do with Daphne?"

"Who's Daphne?" asked Sherman Stork.

The White Rabbit Caper

"Fox thinks somebody killed Daphne Rabbit," said Ben Rat.

"Fonnxx cung brong," rumbled Franz Frog.

"I *could* be wrong," said Fred Fox, "but I'm not." He pulled open the cloakroom door at the bottom of the steps, and the dead body of a female white rabbit toppled furrily onto the cool green carpet. Her head had been bashed in by a heavy blunt instrument.

"Daphne!" screamed old Mrs. Rabbit, bursting into tears.

"I can't see a thing," said Hoot Owl.

"It's a dead white rabbit," said Ben Rat. "Anybody can see that. You're dumb."

"I'm wise!" said Hoot Owl indignantly. "I know everything."

"Jeeng Crine," moaned Franz Frog. He stared up at the chandelier, his eyes bulging and his mammoth mouth gaping open. All the fireflies were frightened and went out.

The cool green hallway became pitch dark. There was a shriek in the black, and a feathery "plump." The fireflies lighted up to see what had happened. Hoot Owl lay dead on the cool green carpet, his head bashed in by a heavy blunt instrument. Ben Rat, Franz Frog, Sherman Stork, old Mrs. Rabbit, and Fred Fox stared at Hoot Owl. Over the cool green carpet crawled a warm red stain, whose source was the body of Hoot Owl. He lay like a feather duster.

"Murder!" squealed old Mrs. Rabbit.

"Nobody leaves this hallway!" snapped Fred Fox. "There's a killer loose in this club!"

"I am not used to death," said Sherman Stork.

"Roong!" groaned Franz Frog.

"He says he's ruined," said Ben Rat, but Fred Fox wasn't listening. He was looking for a heavy blunt instrument. There wasn't any.

"Search them!" cried old Mrs. Rabbit. "Somebody has a sap, or a sock full of sand, or something!"

"Yeh," said Fred Fox. "Ben Rat is a sap—maybe someone swung him by his tail."

"You oughta go on the stage," snarled Ben Rat.

FRED FOX searched the suspects, but he found no concealed weapon. "You could have strangled them with that muffler," Fred Fox told Sherman Stork.

"But they were not strangled," said Sherman Stork.

Fred Fox turned to Ben Rat. "You could have bitten them to death with your ugly teeth," he said.

"But they weren't bitten to death," said Ben Rat.

Fred Fox stared at Franz Frog. "You could have scared them to death with your ugly face," he said.

"Bung wung screng ta deng," said Franz Frog.

"You're right," admitted Fred Fox. "They weren't. Where's old Mrs. Rabbit?" he asked suddenly.

"I'm hiding in here," called old Mrs. Rabbit from the cloakroom. "I'm frightened."

The White Rabbit Caper

Fred Fox got her out of the cool green sanctuary and went in himself. It was dark. He groped around on the cool green carpet. He didn't know what he was looking for, but he found it, a small object lying in a far corner. He put it in his pocket and came out of the cloakroom.

"What'd you find, shamus?" asked Ben Rat apprehensively.

"Exhibit A," said Fred Fox casually.

"Sahng plang keeng," moaned Franz Frog.

"He says somebody's playing for keeps," said Ben Rat.

"He can say that again," said Fred Fox as the front door was flung open and Inspector Mastiff trotted in, followed by Sergeant Dachshund.

"Well, well, look who's muzzling in," said Fred Fox.

"What have we got here?" barked Inspector Mastiff.

"I hate a private nose," said Sergeant Dachshund.

Fred Fox grinned at him. "What happened to your legs from the knees down, sport?" he asked.

"Drop dead," snarled Sergeant Dachshund.

"Quiet, both of you!" snapped Inspector Mastiff. "I know Ollie Owl, but who's the twenty-dollar Easter present from Schrafft's?" He turned on Fred Fox. "If this bunny's head comes off and she's filled with candy, I'll have your badge, Fox," he growled.

"She's real, Inspector," said Fred Fox. "Real dead, too. How did you pick up the scent?"

Inspector Mastiff howled. "The Sergeant thought he smelled a rat at the Lily Club," he said. "Wrong again, as usual. Who's this dead rabbit?"

"She's my great-great-great-great-great-grand-daughter," sobbed old Mrs. Rabbit.

Fred Fox lighted a cigarette. "Oh, no, she isn't, sweetheart," he said coolly. "You are *her* great-great-great-great-great-granddaughter." Pink lightning flared in the live white rabbit's eyes. "You killed the old lady, so you could take over her carrot farm," continued Fred Fox, "and then you killed Hoot Owl."

"I'll kill you, too, shamus!" shrieked Daphne Rabbit.

"Put the cuffs on her, Sergeant," barked Inspector Mastiff. Sergeant Dachshund put a pair of handcuffs on the front legs of the dead rabbit. "Not *her,* you dumb kraut!" yelped Inspector Mastiff. It was too late. Daphne Rabbit had jumped through a window-pane and run away, with the Sergeant in hot pursuit.

"ALL WHITE RABBITS look alike to me," growled Inspector Mastiff. "How could you tell them apart—from their ears?"

"No," said Fred Fox. "From their years. The white rabbit that called on me darn near beat me to the Lily Pad, and no old woman can do that."

The White Rabbit Caper

"Don't brag," said Inspector Mastiff. "Spryness isn't enough. What else?"

"She understood expressions an old rabbit doesn't know," said Fred Fox, "like 'hop the hutch' and 'throb' and 'skip it' and 'sap.' "

"You can't hang a rabbit for her vocabulary," said Inspector Mastiff. "Come again."

Fred Fox pulled the snapshot out of his pocket. "The white rabbit who called on me told me Daphne was eighteen months old," he said, "but read what it says on the back of this picture."

Inspector Mastiff took the snapshot, turned it over, and read, " 'Daphne on her second birthday.' "

"Yes," said Fred Fox. "Daphne knocked six months off her age. You see, Inspector, she couldn't read the writing on the snapshot, because those weren't her spectacles she was wearing."

"Now wait a minute," growled Inspector Mastiff. "Why did she kill Hoot Owl?"

"Elementary, my dear Mastiff," said Fred Fox. "Hoot Owl lived in an oak tree, and she was afraid he saw her burrowing into the club last night, dragging Grandma. She heard Hoot Owl say, 'I'm wise. I know everything,' and so she killed him."

"What with?" demanded the Inspector.

"Her right hind foot," said Fred Fox. "I was looking for a concealed weapon, and all the time she was carrying her heavy blunt instrument openly."

"Well, what do you know!" exclaimed Inspector Mastiff. "Do you think Hoot Owl really saw her?"

"Could be," said Fred Fox. "I happen to think he was bragging about his wisdom in general and not about a particular piece of information, but your guess is as good as mine."

"What did you pick up in the cloakroom?" squeaked Ben Rat.

"The final strand in the rope that will hang Daphne," said Fred Fox. "I knew she didn't go in there to hide. She went in there to look for something she lost last night. If she'd been frightened, she would have hidden when the flies went out, but she went in there after the flies lighted up again."

"That adds up," said Inspector Mastiff grudgingly. "What was it she was looking for?"

"Well," said Fred Fox, "she heard something drop in the dark when she dragged Grandma in there last night and she thought it was a button, or a buckle, or a bead, or a bangle, or a brooch that would incriminate her. That's why she rang me in on the case. She couldn't come here alone to look for it."

"Well, what was it, Fox?" snapped Inspector Mastiff.

"A carrot," said Fred Fox, and he took it out of his pocket, "probably fell out of old Mrs. Rabbit's reticule, if you like irony."

The White Rabbit Caper

"One more question," said Inspector Mastiff. "Why plant the body in the Lily Pad?"

"Easy," said Fred Fox. "She wanted to throw suspicion on the Croaker, a well-known lady-killer."

"Nawng," rumbled Franz Frog.

"Well, there it is, Inspector," said Fred Fox, "all wrapped up for you and tied with ribbons."

Ben Rat disappeared into a wall. Franz Frog hopped back to his office.

"Mercy!" cried Sherman Stork. "I'm late for an appointment!" He flew to the front door and opened it.

There stood Daphne Rabbit, holding the unconscious form of Sergeant Dachshund. "I give up," she said. "I surrender."

"Is he dead?" asked Inspector Mastiff hopefully.

"No," said Daphne Rabbit. "He fainted."

"I never have any luck," growled Inspector Mastiff.

Fred Fox leaned over and pointed to Daphne's right hind foot. "Owl feathers," he said. "She's all yours, Inspector."

"Thanks, Fox," said Inspector Mastiff. "I'll throw something your way someday."

"Make it a nice, plump Plymouth Rock pullet," said Fred Fox, and he sauntered out of the Lily Pad.

BACK IN HIS OFFICE, Fred Fox dictated his report on the White Rabbit Caper to his secretary, Lura Fox.

"Period. End of report," he said finally, toying with the emerald stickpin he had taken from Franz Frog's green necktie when the fireflies went out.

"Is she pretty?" asked Lura Fox.

"Daphne? Quite a dish," said Fred Fox, "but I like my rabbits stewed, and I'm afraid little Daphne is going to fry."

"But she's so young, Fred!" cried Lura Fox. "Only eighteen months!"

"You weren't listening," said Fred Fox.

"How did you know she wasn't interested in Franz Frog?" asked Lura Fox.

"Simple," said Fred Fox. "Wrong species."

"What became of the candy, Fred?" asked Lura Fox.

Fred Fox stared at her. "What candy?" he asked blankly.

Lura Fox suddenly burst into tears. "She was so soft, and warm, and cuddly, Fred," she wailed.

Fred Fox filled a glass with rye, drank it slowly, set down the glass, and sighed grimly. "Sour racket," he said.

CHAPTER FOUR

Back Home Again

WHEN I ARRIVED in Bermuda earlier this year, to catch the weather of April and May, a product of the island that is not exportable, I had a portable radio with me. I had taken it by car to New York, by ship to Hamilton, and by taxi to Paget, carrying it myself, holding it carefully so that it would not be joggled, as if it were an arm in a sling or a spaniel pup. Six weeks later, I carried it back home to Connecticut, never having turned it on while I was away. I don't know why I had taken it with me, since it doesn't work very well anywhere, at sea level or high up in the mountains of Virginia, or not so high in the foothills of the Berkshires.

I have never had a portable radio that worked very well for me. I say "for me" because other people can often make my radio go when I can't. I have what some of my friends call a "dead thumb." When I apply it to the knob of a radio set, there is a curious mechanical resistance. The box either goes completely dead, or gives a high whiny sound, like "squee-ee-een," or says "thog, thog, thog," and stops. Now and then I get a few bars of disconsolate banjo music, from some imaginary station, but that's all. One smart-looking portable I bought in Hollywood ten years ago played all right for a week and then began to go "spreet" or "awp awp" when I clicked the knob. I found out, after wrestling with it, that it would work properly only on its back on the floor. That is, it worked properly on its back for a week. Then it would only go if it were set on something higher than my head. Such a place is hard to find in the average, or normal, house. A housewife objects to a radio that has to be set on the mantelpiece, or hung from the ceiling, or placed on a step halfway up the front stairs. In the end the thing would only play if I held it in my hand.

Back Home Again

This is an uncomfortable way to listen to a concert or a ball game. Your wrist gets numb.

A month and a half away from the American radio is like a year in Arcady. I think such a holiday from Winchell, Just Plain Bill, Pearson, and Milton Berle would cure Network Look, so common in the housewife who turns the radio on when she gets up and lets it run until she goes to bed. This Look is marked by an adenoidal dropping open of the mouth and a vacancy in the eyes, as if perception had just moved out of the mind. The effect of continuous sound from dawn till night may become one of the psychiatrist's chief concerns in this noisy era of man on earth. It is interesting and dismaying to realize that cops, giving a prisoner the third degree, can shatter his nerves more easily with the creaking of a swivel chair than with the glaring of a light. Ours is an age of the power and fear of sound. Already it has its rumors and legends, and even ghost stories. A few years ago there was a terrible and new noise over the city of Brooklyn. Millions of people heard it and were frightened. Nobody could tell where it came from or what caused it. It has not been heard again, but some of the more apprehensive residents of the fabulous borough cock an ear every now and then in broad daylight, or wake on windy nights, and say "Hark!" "Shut up," their wives reply, "and go to sleep." In Brooklyn—oh, anywhere, for that matter—the female of the species is less fearful than the male.

Several years ago I put old Thog Thog, the neurotic Hollywood portable, in the hall closet with my roller skates, my mandolin and my checker board. Old Squeen, the box I took to Bermuda, is now at the radio repair shop. "Here she is again, eh?" said the man when I handed her to him over the counter. "Here she is again," I said. I have little use for the portable when I am home, as I have a cabinet Magnavox in the living room. It works fine and, in accordance with its name, it has a great voice. The man who sold it to me in New York said, "Listen to the volume"—he seemed to think that what I was after was volume. He turned her up as high as she would go, and Brahms' second symphony was bawled out strongly enough to be heard twelve blocks away. "She's powerful, all right!" I shouted over the racket. "Isn't she, though!" screamed the salesman. "Turn her down!" I shrieked, finally. "What?" he howled. I walked over and turned her down.

It was a Sunday when I got back to my house in the country. I turned on the Magnavox, keeping her low, and pushed a station button at random. "Today," said a man's voice, "is the birthday of Bob Hope, Beatrice Lillie, Patrick Henry, and King Charles the Second of England." Yes, I was back home, all right. The man went on to tell about other birthdays of other famous figures. If I am ever stuck for a topic of conversation at dinner, I can turn to the lady on my right and remark, "Rosalind Russell and King George the Third were born on the same day—June the second, if my memory serves." I don't know what my table companion could reply to this, beyond a polite "Indeed" or an impolite "So what?" but I would have made my effort and I could then return to my soup and my private contemplation.

If interesting coincidences of birth do not seem to fascinate your neighbor at table, here are some provocative facts I have gleaned from the "Answer Man" and other radio sources. The porpoise is not mute, but makes a sound like chickens cackling; candles will not drip if you freeze them in the refrigerator before lighting; the Buckeye butterfly of New England kills wasps and small birds but will not take on an adult rabbit; parrots sometimes live to be ninety, but the average life of a steel rail is only twenty years; you can remove rust stains from a washbowl with a piece of lemon; turtles have brown tongues; there are fifty thousand miles of streets in greater New York; milk should be heated in the dark—by wives, not husbands, who are sure to scald themselves severely. I have had my greatest success with the casual query, "Madam, do you know how to take blood stains out of a buffalo robe?" No woman ever lets that go by without comment. "How in the world do you know that?" she will exclaim, or "How on earth did you get blood stains on your buffalo robe?" This last is a neat test of your powers of invention. My own story is that my grandfather, a man of tender honor and quick temper, fired at a knave who had winked at my grandmother during a Hallowe'en party. Grandfather shot the villain as he rode off in his sleigh. "But," one eager lady reminded me, "the bloodstains must have been on the other man's buffalo robe." Don't let this get you. It didn't get me. "My grandfather was sorry," I explained, "so he took the bloodstains out of his victim's buffalo robe, as a sign of his remorse. It turned out the man had not winked at my grandmother, he had merely got something in his eye." "Well, Mr. Thurber," several ladies have asked me, "how *do* you get blood stains out of a buffalo robe?" As a matter of fact, I have forgotten, but I always say quietly, "You soak it, dear lady, in fifteen gallons of milk."

CHAPTER FIVE

My Own Ten Rules for a Happy Marriage

NOBODY, I HASTEN to announce, has asked me to formulate a set of rules for the perpetuation of marital bliss and the preservation of the tranquil American boudoir and inglenook. The idea just came to me one day, when I watched a couple in an apartment across the court from mine gesturing and banging tables and throwing *objets d'art* at each other. I couldn't hear what they were saying, but it was obvious, as the shot-put followed the hammer throw, that he and/or she (as the lawyers would put it) had deeply offended her and/or him.

Their apartment, before they began to take it apart, had been quietly and tastefully arranged, but it was a little hard to believe this now, as he stood there by the fireplace, using an andiron to bat back the Royal Doulton figurines she was curving at him from her strongly entrenched position behind the davenport. I wondered what had started the exciting but costly battle, and, brooding on the general subject of Husbands and Wives, I found myself compiling my own Ten Rules for a Happy Marriage.

I have avoided the timeworn admonitions, such as "Praise her new hat," "Share his hobbies," "Be a sweetheart as well as a wife," and "Don't keep a blonde in the guest room," not only because they are threadbare from repetition, but also because they don't seem to have accomplished their purpose. Maybe what we need is a brand-new set of rules. Anyway, ready or not, here they come, the result of fifty years (I began as a little boy) spent in studying the nature and behavior, mistakes and misunderstandings, of the American Male (*homo Americansis*) and his Mate.

RULE ONE: Neither party to a sacred union should run down, disparage or badmouth the other's former girls

My Own Ten Rules for a Happy Marriage

or beaux, as the case may be. The tendency to attack the character, looks, intelligence, capability and achievements of one's mate's former friends of the opposite sex is a common cause of domestic discontent. Sweetheart-slurring, as we will call this deplorable practice, is encouraged by a long spell of gloomy weather, too many highballs, hang-overs, and the suspicion that one's spouse is hiding, and finding, letters in a hollow tree, or is intercepting the postman, or putting in secret phone calls from the corner drugstore. These fears almost always turn out to be unfounded, but the unfounded fear, as we all know, is worse than the founded.

Aspersions, insinuations, reflections or just plain cracks about old boy friends and girl friends should be avoided at all times. Here are some of the expressions that should be especially eschewed: "That waffle-fingered, minor-league third baseman you latched onto at Cornell"; "You know the girl I mean—the one with the hips who couldn't read"; "That old flame of yours with the vocabulary of a hoot owl"; and "You remember her—that old bat who chewed gum and dressed like Daniel Boone."

This kind of derogatory remark, if persisted in by one or both parties to a marriage, will surely lead to divorce or, at best, a blow on the head with a glass ash tray.

RULE TWO: A man should make an honest effort to get the names of his wife's friends right. This is not easy. The average wife who was graduated from college at any time during the past thirty years keeps in close touch with at least seven old classmates. These ladies, known as "the girls," are named, respectively: Mary, Marian, Melissa, Marjorie, Maribel, Madeleine and Miriam; and all of them are called Myrtle by the careless husband we are talking about. Furthermore, he gets their nicknames wrong. This, to be sure, is understandable, since their nicknames are, respectively: Molly, Muffy, Missy, Midge, Mabby, Maddy and Mims. The careless husband, out of thoughtlessness or pure cussedness, calls them all Mugs, or, when he is feeling particularly brutal, Mucky.

All the girls are married, one of them to a Ben Tompkins, and as this is the only one he can remember, our hero calls all the husbands Ben, or Tompkins, adding to the general annoyance and confusion.

If you are married to a college graduate, then, try to get the names of her girl friends and their husbands straight. This will prevent some of those interminable arguments that begin after Midge and Harry (not Mucky and Ben) have said a stiff good night and gone home.

RULE THREE: A husband should not insult his wife publicly, at parties. He should insult her in the pri-

My Own Ten Rules for a Happy Marriage

vacy of the home. Thus, if a man thinks the soufflés his wife makes are as tough as an outfielder's glove, he should tell her so when they are at home, not when they are out at a formal dinner party where a perfect soufflé has just been served. The same rule applies to the wife. She should not regale his men friends, or women friends, with hilarious accounts of her husband's clumsiness, remarking that he dances like a 1907 Pope Hartford, or that he locked himself in the children's rabbit pen and couldn't get out. All parties must end finally, and the husband or wife who has revealed all may find that there is hell to pay in the taxi going home.

RULE FOUR: The wife who keeps saying, "Isn't that just like a man?" and the husband who keeps saying, "Oh, well, you know how women are," are likely to grow farther and farther apart through the years. These famous generalizations have the effect of reducing an individual to the anonymous status of a mere unit in a mass. The wife who, just in time, comes upon her husband about to fry an egg in a dry skillet should not classify him with all other males but should give him the accolade of a special distinction. She might say, for example, "George, no other man in the world would try to do a thing like that." Similarly, a husband watching his wife laboring to start the car without turning on the ignition should not say to the

My Own Ten Rules for a Happy Marriage

should not lunge instantly into some irrelevant subject. It's wiser to exclaim, "How interesting!" or, at the very least, "Well, well!" She might even compliment him on his diction and his grasp of politics, elm blight or boxing. If he should ask some shrewd question to test her attention, she can cry, "Good heavens!" leap up, and rush out to the kitchen on some urgent fictitious errand. This may fool him, or it may not. I hope, for her sake—and his—that it does.

RULE SIX: A husband should try to remember where things are around the house so that he does not have to wait for his wife to get home from the hairdresser's before he can put his hands on what he wants. Among the things a husband is usually unable to locate are the iodine, the aspirin, the nail file, the French vermouth, his cuff links, studs, black silk socks and evening shirts, the snapshots taken at Nantucket last summer, his favorite recording of "Kentucky Babe," the borrowed copy of *My Cousin Rachel,* the garage key, his own towel, the last bill from Brooks Bros., his pipe cleaners, the poker chips, crackers, cheese, the whetstone, his new raincoat and the screens for the upstairs windows.

I don't really know the solution to this problem, but one should be found. Perhaps every wife should draw for her husband a detailed map of the house, showing clearly the location of everything he might need.

Trouble is, I suppose, he would lay the map down somewhere and not be able to find it until his wife got home.

RULE SEVEN: If a husband is not listening to what his wife is saying, he should not grunt, "Okay" or "Yeah, sure," or make little affirmative noises. A husband lost in thought or worry is likely not to take in the sense of such a statement as this: "We're going to the Gordons' for dinner tonight, John, so I'm letting the servants off. Don't come home from the office first. Remember, we both have to be at the dentist's at five, and I'll pick you up there with the car." Now, an "Okay" or a "Yeah, sure" at this point can raise havoc if the husband hasn't really been listening. As usual, he goes all the way out to his home in Glenville— thirteen miles from the dentist's office and seventeen miles from the Gordons' house—and he can't find his wife. He can't find the servants. His wife can't get him on the phone because all she gets is the busy buzz. John is calling everybody he can think of except, of course, in his characteristic way, the dentist and the Gordons. At last he hangs up, exhausted and enraged. Then the phone rings. It is his wife. And here let us leave them.

RULE EIGHT: If your husband ceases to call you "Sugarfoot" or "Candy Eyes" or "Cutie Fudge Pie" dur-

My Own Ten Rules for a Happy Marriage

ing the first year of your marriage, it is not necessarily a sign that he has come to take you for granted or that he no longer cares. It is probably an indication that he has recovered his normal perspective. Many a young husband who once called his wife "Tender Mittens" or "Taffy Ears" or "Rose Lips" has become austere or important, like a Common Pleas Judge, and he wouldn't want reports of his youthful frivolity to get around. If he doesn't call you Dagmar when your name is Daisy, you are sitting pretty.

RULE NINE: For those whose husbands insist on pitching for the Married Men against the Single Men at the Fourth-of-July picnic of the First M. E. Church, I have the following suggestion: don't sit on the sidelines and watch him. Get lost. George is sure to be struck out by a fourteen-year-old boy, pull up with a charley horse running to first, and get his teeth knocked out by an easy grounder to the mound. When you see him after the game, tell him everybody knew the little boy was throwing illegal spitballs, everybody saw the first baseman spike George, and everybody said that grounder took such a nasty bounce even Phil Rizzuto couldn't have fielded it. Remember, most middle-aged husbands get to sleep at night by imagining they are striking out the entire batting order of the Yankees.

Thurber Country

RULE TEN: A wife's dressing table should be inviolable. It is the one place in the house a husband should get away from and stay away from. And yet, the average husband is drawn to it as by a magnet, especially when he is carrying something wet, oily, greasy or sticky, such as a universal joint, a hub cap, or the blades of a lawn mower. His excuse for bringing these alien objects into his wife's bedroom in the first place is that he is looking for "an old rag" with which to wipe them off. There are no old rags in a lady's boudoir, but husbands never seem to learn this. They search hampers, closets and bureau drawers, expecting to find a suitable piece of cloth, but first they set the greasy object on the dressing table. The aggrieved wife may be tempted, following this kind of vandalism, to lock her bedroom door and kick her husband out for good. I suggest, however, a less stringent punishment. Put a turtle in his bed. The wife who is afraid to pick up a turtle should ask Junior to help her. Junior will love it.

Now I realize, in glancing back over these rules, that some of my solutions to marital problems may seem a little untidy; that I have, indeed, left a number of loose ends here and there. For example, if the husbands are going to mislay their detailed maps of household objects, I have accomplished nothing except to add one item for the distraught gentleman to lose.

My Own Ten Rules for a Happy Marriage

Then, there is that turtle. Captious critics will point out that a turtle in a husband's bed is not a valid solution to anything, but merely a further provocation. The outraged husband will deliberately trip his wife during their next mixed-doubles match. She will thereupon retaliate by putting salt in his breakfast coffee. . . .

Let somebody else try to figure out what to do about the Running Feud in marriage. The Williamses are coming to dinner tonight, and I promised to put the white wine on the ice at three o'clock. It is now six-thirty. After all, I have my own problems.

CHAPTER SIX

What a Lovely Generalization!

I HAVE COLLECTED, in my time, derringers, snow-storm paperweights, and china and porcelain dogs, and perhaps I should explain what happened to these old collections before I go on to my newest hobby, which is the true subject of this monograph. My derringer collection may be regarded as having been discontinued, since I collected only two, the second and last item as long ago as 1935. There were originally seventeen snowstorm paperweights, but only four or five are left. This kind of collection is known to the expert as a "diminished collection," and it is not considered cricket to list it in your *Who's Who* biography. The snowstorm paperweight suffers from its easy appeal to the eye and the hand. House guests like to play with paperweights and to slip them into their luggage while packing up to leave. As for my china and porcelain dogs, I disposed of that collection some two years ago. I had decided that the

What a Lovely Generalization!

collection of actual objects, of any kind, was too much of a strain, and I determined to devote myself, instead, to the impalpable and the intangible.

Nothing in my new collection can be broken or stolen or juggled or thrown at cats. What I collect now is a certain kind of Broad Generalization, or Sweeping Statement. You will see what I mean when I bring out some of my rare and cherished pieces. All you need to start a collection of generalizations like mine is an attentive ear. Listen in particular to women, whose average generalization is from three to five times as broad as a man's. Generalizations, male or female, may be true ("Women don't sleep very well"), untrue ("There are no pianos in Japan"), half true ("People would rather drink than go to the theater"), debatable ("Architects have the wrong idea"), libellous ("Doctors don't know what they're doing"), ridiculous ("You never see foreigners fishing"), fascinating but undemonstrable ("People who break into houses don't drink wine"), or idiosyncratic ("Peach ice cream is never as good as you think it's going to be").

"There are no pianos in Japan" was the first item in my collection. I picked it up at a reception while discussing an old movie called "The Battle," or "Thunder in the East," which starred Charles Boyer, Merle Oberon, and John Loder, some twenty years ago. In one scene, Boyer, as a Japanese naval captain,

comes upon Miss Oberon, as his wife, Matsuko, playing an old Japanese air on the piano for the entertainment of Loder, a British naval officer with a dimple,
who has forgotten more about fire control, range finding, marksmanship, and lovemaking than the Japanese
commander is ever going to know. "Matsuko," says the
latter, "why do you play that silly little song? It may
be tedious for our fran." Their fran, John Loder, says,
"No, it is, as a matter of—" But I don't know why I
have to go into the whole plot. The lady with whom
I was discussing the movie, at the reception, said that
the detail about Matsuko and the piano was absurd,
since "there are no pianos in Japan." It seems that this
lady was an authority on the musical setup in Japan
because her great-uncle had married a singsong girl
in Tokyo in 1912.

Now, I might have accepted the declarations that
there are no saxophones in Bessarabia, no banjo-
mandolins in Mozambique, no double basses in Zanzibar, no jew's-harps in Rhodesia, no zithers in Mad-
agascar, and no dulcimers in Milwaukee, but I could
not believe that Japan, made out in the movie as a
great imitator of Western culture, would not have any
pianos. Some months after the reception, I picked up
an old copy of the *Saturday Evening Post* and, in an
article on Japan, read that there were, before the war,
some fifteen thousand pianos in Japan. It just happened to say that, right there in the article.

What a Lovely Generalization!

You may wonder where I heard some of the other Sweeping Statements I have mentioned above. Well, the one about peach ice cream was contributed to my collection by a fifteen-year-old girl. I am a chocolate man myself, but the few times I have eaten peach ice cream it tasted exactly the way I figured it was going to taste, which is why I classify this statement as idiosyncratic; that is, peculiar to one individual. The item about foreigners never fishing, or, at any rate, never fishing where you can see them, was given to me last summer by a lady who had just returned from a motor trip through New England. The charming generalization about people who break into houses popped out of a conversation I overheard between two women, one of whom said it was not safe to leave rye, Scotch, or bourbon in your summer house when you closed it for the winter, but it was perfectly all right to leave your wine, since intruders are notoriously men of insensitive palate, who cannot tell the difference between Nuits-St.-Georges and saddle polish. I would not repose too much confidence in this theory if I were you, however. It is one of those Comfortable Conclusions that can cost you a whole case of Château Lafite.

I HAVEN'T got space here to go through my entire collection, but there is room to examine a few more items. I'm not sure where I got hold of "Gamblers hate women"—possibly at Bleeck's—but, like "Sopranos drive men crazy," it has an authentic ring. This is not true, I'm afraid, of "You can't trust an electrician" or "Cops off duty always shoot somebody." There may be something in "Dogs know when you're despondent" and "Sick people hear everything," but I sharply question the validity of "Nobody taps his fingers if he's all right" and "People who like birds are queer."

Some twenty years ago, a Pittsburgh city editor came out with the generalization that "Rewrite men go crazy when the moon is full," but this is perhaps a little too special for the layman, who probably doesn't know what a rewrite man is. Besides, it is the abusive type of Sweeping Statement and should not be dignified by analysis or classification.

In conclusion, let us briefly explore "Generals are afraid of their daughters," vouchsafed by a lady after I had told her my General Wavell anecdote. It happens, for the sake of our present record, that the late General Wavell, of His Britannic Majesty's forces, discussed his three daughters during an interview a few years ago. He said that whereas he had millions of men under his command who leaped at his every order, he couldn't get his daughters down to breakfast on time when he was home on leave, in spite of stern directives issued the night before. As I have imagined it, his ordeal went something like this. It would get to be 7 A.M., and then 7:05, and General Wavell would shout up the stairs demanding to know

What a Lovely Generalization!

where everybody was, and why the girls were not at table. Presently, one of them would call back sharply, as a girl has to when her father gets out of hand, "For heaven's sake, Daddy, will you be quiet! Do you want to wake the neighbors?" The General, his flanks rashly exposed, so to speak, would fall back in orderly retreat and eat his kippers by himself. Now, I submit that there is nothing in this to prove that the General was afraid of his daughters. The story merely establishes the fact that his daughters were not afraid of him.

If you are going to start collecting Sweeping Statements on your own, I must warn you that certain drawbacks are involved. You will be inclined to miss the meaning of conversations while lying in wait for generalizations. Your mouth will hang open slightly, your posture will grow rigid, and your eyes will take on the rapt expression of a person listening for the faint sound of distant sleigh bells. People will avoid your company and whisper that you are probably an old rewrite man yourself or, at best, a finger tapper who is a long way from being all right. But your collection will be a source of comfort in your declining years, when you can sit in the chimney corner cackling the evening away over some such gems, let us say, as my own two latest acquisitions: "Jewellers never go anywhere" and "Intellectual women dress funny."

Good hunting.

CHAPTER SEVEN

The Interview

W ONDERFUL PLACE you have here," said the man
from the newspaper. He stood with his host
on a rise of ground from where, down a slope to the
right, they could see a dead garden, killed by winter,
and, off to the left, spare, grim trees stalking the ghost
of a brook.

"Everybody says that," said George Lockhorn.
"Everybody says it's a wonderful place, to which I

The Interview

used to reply 'Thank you,' or 'I'm glad you think so,' or 'Yes, it is, isn't it?' At fifty-eight, Price, I say what I know. I say that you and the others are, by God, debasing the word wonderful. This bleak prospect is no more wonderful than a frozen shirt. Even in full summer it's no more wonderful than an unfrozen shirt. I will give you the synonyms for wonderful—wondrous, miraculous, prodigious, astonishing, amazing, phenomenal, unique, curious, strange. I looked them up an hour ago, because I knew you would say this is a wonderful place. Apply any of those words to that dahlia stalk down there."

"I see what you mean," said Price, who was embarrassed, and began looking in his pockets for something that wasn't there.

"I have known only a few wonderful things in my fifty-eight years," said Lockhorn. "They are easy to enumerate, since I have been practicing up to toss them off to you casually: the body of a woman, the works of a watch, the verses of Keats, the structure of the hyacinth, the devotion of the dog. Trouble is, I tossed those off casually for the St. Louis *Post-Dispatch* man, or the Rochester *Times-Union* man. It's cold out here. Shall we go inside?"

"Just as you say," said the interviewer, who had reached for the copy paper and the pencil in his pocket, but didn't bring them out. "It's bracing out here, though."

"You're freezing to death, without your hat and overcoat, and you know it," said Lockhorn. "It's late enough for a highball— Do you drink cocktails?"

"No, sir. That is, not often," said Price.

"You're probably a liar," Lockhorn said. "Everybody replies to my questions the way they think I want them to reply. You can say that I say 'everybody-they'; I hate 'everybody-he.' 'Has everybody brought his or her slate?' a teacher of mine, a great goat of a woman, used to ask us. There is no other tongue in the world as clumsy as ours is—with its back to certain corners. That's been used, too—and don't make notes, or don't let me see you make notes. Never made a note in my life, except after a novel was finished. Plot the chapters out, outline the characters after the book has been published."

"That is extremely interesting," said Price. "What do you do with the notes?"

They had reached the rear of the house now. "We'll go in the back way," said Lockhorn. "I keep them around, tuck them away where my executor can find them if he's on his toes. This is the woodshed. We'll go through the kitchen. Some of my best character touches, some of the best devices, too, are in the notes. Anybody can write a novel, but it takes talent to do notes. We'll go through this door."

"This is wonderful," said Price. "I'm sorry. I mean—"

The Interview

"Let it stand," said Lockhorn. "Wonderful in the sense of being astonishing, curious, and strange. Don't take the chair by the fire," he added as they reached the living room. "That's mine."

LOCKHORN DROPPED into the chair by the fireplace and motioned his guest into another. "Can I use that about the notes?" asked Price. "Mr. Hammer wants something new."

"Make us both a drink," Lockhorn said. "That's a bar over there. I drink bourbon, but there's Scotch and rye, too."

"I'll have bourbon," said Price.

"Everybody has what I have," Lockhorn growled. "I said Scotch, and the *Times-Union* man had Scotch; I said rye, and the *Post-Dispatch* man had rye. No, you can't use that about the notes. Tell it to everybody. Beginning to believe it myself. Have you gained the idea in your half hour here that I am a maniac?"

Price, noisily busy with bottles and glasses, laughed uncomfortably. "Everybody knows that your methods of work are unusual," he said. "May I ask what you are working on now?"

"Easy on the soda," said Lockhorn. "Martha will raise hell when she finds me drinking. Just bow at her and grin."

Price put two frightened squirts of soda in one glass

and filled up the other. "Mrs. Lockhorn?" he asked, handing the strong highball to his host.

"What is this man Hammer like?" Lockhorn demanded. "No, let me tell you. He says 'remotely resembles,' he says 'flashes of insight.' He begins, by God, sentences with 'moreover.' I had an English teacher who began sentences with 'too.' 'Too, there are other factors to be considered.' The man says he's read Macaulay, but he never got past page six—Hammer, that is. Should have gone into real estate—subdivisions, opening up suburbs, and so on. This English teacher started every class by saying, 'None of us can write.' Hadn't been for that man, I would have gone into real estate—subdivisions, opening up suburbs, and so on. But he was a challenge. You can say my memoirs will be called 'I Didn't Want to Write.'" Lockhorn had almost finished his drink. "I'll have to see a proof," he said. "I'll have to see a proof of your article. Have you noticed that everybody says everything twice? They say everything twice. 'Yes, they do,' you'll say. 'Yes, they do.' Only contribution I've made to literature is the discovery of the duplicate statement. 'How the hell are you, Bill?' a guy will say. 'How the hell are you, anyway?' 'Fine,' Bill will say. 'Just fine.'"

"That's very interesting," said Price, and, feeling that his host expected it, he added, "That's very interesting."

The Interview

Lockhorn held out his glass and Price carried it back to the bar. "The *Times* man, or whoever it was," Lockhorn went on, "put down that one of the things I regard as wonderful is the feminine anatomy. You can't get 'body of a woman' in the papers. The feminine anatomy is something that can be touched only with the mind, and you'll notice that in my list everything can be touched by the hand. A watch a man never held would not be wonderful."

"That's true," said Price, speculating on the tactual aspect of devotion.

"There is only one thing I've never told an interviewer," Lockhorn said, after a pause. "I've never told any interviewer about the game. 'Don't tell the man about the game,' Mrs. Lockhorn always says. 'Promise me you won't tell the man about the game.' Let me ask you one thing—why would Martha ask me not to tell you about the game if there were no game?"

"She wouldn't, of course," said Price, taking a long slow sip of his drink to cover his embarrassment. The two men drank in silence for a while. "My second wife left me because of the game," Lockhorn said, "but you can't print that, because she would deny it, and I would deny it." Lockhorn took a great gulp of his drink and stared into the fire again. Two minutes of silence went by, during which Price found himself counting the ticks of the clock on the mantelpiece. "My memory is beginning to slip," Lockhorn said, "but if you print that, I'll sue Hammer's pants off. Maybe I'll sue his pants off anyway. Sunday editors are the worst vermin in the world. If you use that, credit it to Mencken. I don't know why the hell you boys want to interview me. I've said a great many sharp things in my life, but I can't remember which ones are mine and which ones were said by Santayana or John Jay Chapman. You can say my memory is slipping—maybe it will arouse pity. I'm the loneliest man in the United States." Lockhorn had finished his drink very fast, and he got up and walked to the bar. Price's eyebrows went up as he heard the heavy slug of bourbon chortle into the glass. "Martha'll be sore as a pup," Lockhorn said with an owlish grin. "Just touch your forelock to her. You can't argue with her. She's my fourth wife, you know. The others were Dorothy, Nettie, and Pauline, not necessarily in that order." He came back to his chair and flopped into it. Price began to listen to the clock again. Lockhorn's head jerked up suddenly. "Going to call my memoirs 'I Had to Write,'" he said. "You can put that in your piece if you want to."

WHEN MRS. LOCKHORN came into the room, smiling her small, apprehensive smile, Price had just handed his host a seventh highball. "This is Pricey," said Lockhorn. Price, who had jumped to his feet, stood bowing and grinning at his hostess. She barely touched him with her smile. "One for the house," said Lockhorn, holding up his drink.

"It's early," said Mrs. Lockhorn. "It isn't five yet."

"I must be going," Price said. "May I make you a drink, Mrs. Lockhorn?"

"No, thank you," she said, in a tone that corked the bottles.

"Nonsense," said Lockhorn. "Sit down, Pricey. I've never, by God, known anything like the female timetable. They live by the clock. The purpose of 6 P.M. is to unlock their inhibitions about liquor. Sexual intercourse is for holidays—"

"George!" said Mrs. Lockhorn sharply.

Price began to babble. "Well, I guess it was us men —we men—who actually set a schedule for drinking, with that business about the sun over the yardarm, wasn't it, Mr. Lockhorn?"

"Sun over your grandma's thigh," said Lockhorn irritably, looking at Price but aiming the phrase at his wife. "Who called tea 'the five o'clock'? Women, French women. They don't even believe a man should smoke until he puts on his tuxedo. We are a prisoner of the hours, Pricey, and you know it." Price flushed and became vastly conscious of his hands.

"Finish your drink," said Martha Lockhorn to Price. "My husband is going to finish his, and then I'm afraid he must rest. The new book has taken a great deal out of him."

"You're goddam tootin' he's going to finish his," said Lockhorn, his fingers whitening on his glass, "and don't third-person me. Sit down, Pricey. We're just getting started." Price sat stiffly on the edge of his chair. He saw that Mrs. Lockhorn, who had moved behind her husband's chair, was trying to communicate with him by a shake of her head and a glance at the bar. "Don't let 'em third-person you, Pricey," said Lockhorn sternly. "Next comes the first person plural —they first-person-plural you to death. Then you might just as well go to bed and die. You might just as well go to bed and die."

"I hope he hasn't been entertaining you with imprecations all afternoon," said Mrs. Lockhorn.

"Oh, no indeed," exclaimed Price, picking up his glass and setting it down.

"She loves the happy phrase," said Lockhorn. "She spends more time on phrases than most women do on their hips."

"Don't be tiresome, George," said Mrs. Lockhorn. She turned to Price. "You see, he has been interviewed constantly," she told him. "It seems as if there has been an interviewer here every day since his novel came out. You all want something different, and then it never comes out the way he says it. It's all twisted and ridiculous."

"I hope to avoid that sin," said Price, noting that

the famous author had closed his eyes but still kept his tight grip on his glass.

"He's terribly tired." Mrs. Lockhorn's voice was lowered to a whisper, as if they were in a sickroom. "He worked four years on 'The Flaw in the Crystal.' Some of the reviews have hurt him deeply."

"It's selling wonderfully," whispered Price.

Mrs. Lockhorn made a gesture with her hands, but its meaning was lost on him.

The novelist opened his eyes and quickly finished his drink. "I'll tell you some other wonderful things," he said. "A woman crying, children calling over the snow—across the snow—dogs barking at a distance, dogs barking far off at night." He put his empty glass on the floor and groped in the air for more wonders with his right hand. "Things I've wanted to do," he went on. "You can use this, Pricey. Bat baseballs through the windows of a firescraper from a lower roof across the street, spend—"

"Skyscraper," said Mrs. Lockhorn.

To Price's secret delight his host, after a slow stare at Mrs. Lockhorn, repeated with great authority, "Firescraper." He winked at Price. "I want to spend the night in Ovington's," he said. "I want to open a pigeon. All my life I've wanted to cut a dove open, looking for the goddamnedest omens in the history of the world. Like the Romans performing the ancient assizes. I want to find two hearts in one of the sons of bitches and go crying through the night, like another Whozis, 'Repent, ye sinners, repent. The world is coming to an end.' "

"George," said Mrs. Lockhorn, "the newspapers can't print things like that."

Lockhorn didn't hear her. He picked up the glass and drank the trickle of ice water in it. "Go down, ye sinners, to the sea," he said, with a wide gesture.

"Talk about your book," said his wife. "The newspapers want to know about your book."

Lockhorn looked at her. "They are all the same, Pricey," he said, "and they differ as the waves differ. Only in height. The blood of the dove, as they say, Pricey. I'll tell you about the book, drunk as I unexpectedly am, or get."

"He's terribly tired," cut in his wife.

"Spiritual hope!" bawled Lockhorn, so loudly Price started the ice tinkling in his glass. "Spiritual hope is my tiny stock in trade, to quote the greatest master of them all."

Mrs. Lockhorn, observing that the newspaperman looked puzzled, said, "He means Henry James," and then, to her husband, "I think he spoke of his *small* trade, George."

"The greatest master of them all," said Lockhorn again. "I always begin with a picture, a visual picture. Woman standing in the doorway with the evening sun in her hair. Dying rays of the evening sun in her hair, as Hockett would put it."

"Hockett?" asked Price, realizing, with a small cold feeling in his stomach, that he was not going to have anything to write.

"Your boss," said Lockhorn.

"Oh, Hammer," said Price.

"I beg your pardon?" said Mrs. Lockhorn.

The author jiggled what was left of the ice in his glass. "The women write backwards," he said, "beginning with their titles—'Never Dies the Dream,' 'Lonely Is the Hunting Heart.'"

"It's 'The Heart Is a Lonely Hunter,'" said his wife, but Lockhorn waved her away.

"I'm tired of the adult world seen through the eyes of a little girl," he said. "A woman forgets everything that happens to her after she is fourteen. I, too, have lived in Arcady, Pricey, but I'm tired of viewing the adult world through the great solemn eyes of a sensitive—What is that word like nipper?"

"Moppet?" asked Price.

"Sensitive moppet," said Lockhorn, closing his eyes, and sinking deeper in his chair.

Price attempted to make a surreptitious note on his copy paper.

"You can't use that," whispered Mrs. Lockhorn. "He's talking about one of his closest women friends."

The interviewer put his pencil and paper away as

his host opened his eyes again and pointed a finger at him. "Henry James had the soul of an eavesdropper," he said. Price gave a laugh that did not sound like his own. "Everything he got, he got from what he overheard somebody say. No visual sense, and if you haven't got visual sense, what have you got?"

Price stood up as if to go, but Lockhorn waved him down again and grinned at his wife. "Pricey, here, has invented some remarkable game, Martha," he said. "Tell Martha about your game, son. It's all we've talked about all afternoon."

Price swallowed.

"What sort of game is it?" asked Martha.

"It's nothing, really," gurgled Price. He stood up again. "I must be running along," he said.

"Sit down for a moment," said Mrs. Lockhorn. "George, you better lie down awhile."

To Price's astonishment, the novelist got meekly to his feet and started for the door into the hall. He stopped in front of Price and stuck an index finger into his ribs, making a skucking sound with his tongue. "Is love worse living?" he said, and went out into the hall and closed the door behind him. He began to stomp up the carpeted stairs, shouting, "Dorothy! Nettie! Martha!"

Price, swallowing again, idiotically wondered what ever became of Pauline.

"As you see, he's really worn out," said Mrs. Lock-

The Interview

horn hastily. "He's not as young as he used to be, of course, and I wish he'd give up writing. After all, he's written eighteen books and he has a comfortable income."

From far upstairs Price heard a now faint shouting for the lost Pauline.

"Are you sure you won't have another drink?" asked Mrs. Lockhorn, not moving from the edge of her chair.

"A quick one, perhaps," said Price. "Just half a glass."

"Surely," said Mrs. Lockhorn with the hint of a sigh, taking his glass. "Bourbon?"

"Scotch, if you don't mind," said Price.

She made it very small, and very weak. "I know that you will use discretion," she said. "George has become a little reckless in some of the things he says, and I hope you were able to tell the truth from the things he just makes up."

Price finished half his drink. "I'm afraid I really haven't got anything," he said miserably. "Perhaps you could tell me something I could use."

Mrs. Lockhorn looked mysterious. "There are some wonderful things about the book," she said. "I mean about the way he wrote it and what had to be done by the publishers. He had actually written, word for word, a chapter from one of his earlier books into the new one. He hadn't copied it, you understand. It was simply there in his memory, word for word." Price got out his pencil and paper, but his hostess lifted her hand. "Oh, mercy!" she said. "You can't possibly print that. He would be furious if he found it out."

Price looked puzzled. "If he found it out?" he asked.

She stood up and Price got to his feet. "Oh, he doesn't remember writing it," she said. "It was just stuck in. The publishers had to take it out. But you mustn't mention it. Please don't even tell Mr. Hockett."

Price set his glass down on the table beside his chair. "I believe my hat and overcoat—" he began.

"I'll get them," she said. "They must be in the hall closet."

There was no sound from upstairs. Price got into his coat, and Mrs. Lockhorn went with him to the front door and opened it. "I'm sorry," she said. "I'm afraid it's been something of a wild-goose chase."

"I'm afraid it has," said Price, a little grimly.

Mrs. Lockhorn gave him her best hostess smile. "George gets mixed up when he's tired," she explained, "or he wouldn't have said 'Is love worse living?'"

Price matched her smile with one just as artificial. "He was quoting one of the most famous lines ever written by James Joyce," he said. He went out and got into his car. "Goodbye, Mrs. Lockhorn," he said.

The Interview

"Goodbye, Mr. Pricey," she called to him. Her smile was gone. "I'm sorry you didn't have time to tell me about your game."

"Some other time, maybe," said Price, whose smile was also gone, and he started the engine.

Mrs. Lockhorn closed the front door.

When Price had driven a few hundred yards from the house, he took the copy paper from his pocket and threw it out of the window. Then, suddenly, he reached for his pencil and threw it out of the window, too.

CHAPTER EIGHT

Lady in a Trap

SOMETIMES THOSE little fillers you see in newspapers are more fascinating and provocative than the major news stories, and one of this kind turned up not long ago in the watchful and sympathetic *New York Times*. It went like this: "When a female mole is caught in a trap, the male often worries so much that he starves to death." My wife read this item aloud to me, in a reproachful tone, clearly implying that the male of any species, including mine, would be awkwardly helpless, and just go to pieces, if he came upon his mate caught in a trap, or bound and gagged and locked in the linen closet. I spoke up before she could get off whatever sardonic comment was on the tip of her tongue.

"Devoted little fellow, the ground mole," I said quickly. "Note that he does not seize this golden opportunity to run away with the female chipmunk that lives in the oak tree. No, he stands loyally by, thinking of Mama and grieving over her fate."

"In a tomcat's eye he does," said my wife. "The item does not say 'grieves,' it says 'worries.' It was obviously written by a male. You would think that the male mole was in a worse dilemma than the female. The trouble with the male is—"

"The trouble with the female is that she is constantly walking into traps," I cut in. "I will never forget that awful, cold night on Third Avenue when we couldn't get a cab, and one suddenly drove up from nowhere and stopped, and a man got out of the back seat, held open the door, and said, 'Get in.' Before I could stop you, you got in and I had to follow. It turned out that we were in a gyp cab and that the gallant gentleman who had offered to share his taxi was, in reality, a burglar."

"He was not a burglar, he was only a pickpocket," my wife explained, "and besides, he dropped us at our apartment building, and he didn't steal anything. You are trying to change the subject."

"You were just lucky that night. I managed to get between the guy and you, or he would have had your money and mink. The female should always avoid doors that are held invitingly open, especially those that are held open by a small stick, or by a pickpocket."

Lady in a Trap

"All the male mole thinks about when he finds his mate in a trap," she went on, oblivious of my warning, "is where his next meal is coming from. That isn't his loved one he sees in the trap, it is his cook. The male knows that as soon as he finishes the crackers and milk —and the whiskey—and is faced with the problem of cooking something, he is a gone male. He will starve to death out of ignorance, and not out of sorrow. You surely remember the time that you—"

"I don't want to go through that again," I said, crisply, knowing full well what she was thinking about. She was thinking about the time I poured some dry Wheatena in the top of a double-boiler, filled the bottom part with water, and set the boiler on a gas jet, getting not cereal for breakfast, but only evaporation. My wife and I can never talk about the ineptitude of any male without bringing his faults and flaws down on my own head, but this, I understand from my men friends, is an unfair trick resorted to, in argument, by all wives.

A few days later, when she had driven over to the hairdresser's in Torrington, I decided to make a secret exploration of our pantry and kitchen, so that I could show an easy surprising familiarity with them the next time she said, "A man never knows where anything is." Since it was the cook's day off, I had the house to myself, and I decided to proceed on the assumption that Mama was caught in a trap and that I had to prepare a meal for myself, without help from any female. The experiment proved, to my dismay, that the average husband would be lost in his own kitchen. Let us take not me, but a hypothetical husband named John, whose wife is caught in a trap.

Entering the kitchen, he is instantly surprised by its strangeness, and also by its neatness. He wanders into the pantry and sees a lot of drawers and cupboard doors. The first door he pulls open reveals nothing to eat, but only several shelves containing enough glasses of all kinds, it seems to him, for a family of fifteen—highball glasses, and glasses for sherry, cocktails, wine, and just plain water. The next door opens up to reveal two hundred plates, including the Spode set, and green glass ones for salad. Next he finds himself palely wandering among big, useless platters and formidable tureens. He decides he is up too high and he opens a couple of cupboard doors flush with the floor, and gets tangled up with the things you make onion soup and shirred eggs in, and a lot of iron, copper, and aluminum objects, in a recess that becomes deeper and darker, at the end of which he unearths a waffle iron. He hastily closes these doors and begins pulling out drawers filled with knives and spoons.

At this point, he realizes that he should probably find the refrigerator, which he finally does, peering helplessly inside, getting his forefinger into something cold and sticky, and, at length, removing a head of lettuce wrapped in cheesecloth and two eggs. He sets these on the kitchen table, but the eggs begin to roll, so he puts them in his pocket.

Coffee is now the thing that comes to mind, but all he can find at first is a shelf holding raisins, cream of wheat, corn meal, noodles, rice, Jello, cake flour, Quaker oats, and baking powder. Not far from these he finds vanilla, spices, tabasco sauce, and a bottle of Worcestershire. He now feels that he is losing ground rapidly. Ten minutes later he finds the coffee in a can marked "Coffee," puts it on the kitchen table, takes off the lid, and finds himself, to his astonishment, placing the two eggs in the coffee can, where they will not roll. This, it occurs to him, is somehow wrong, and he remembers Christopher Columbus's solution of the problem of how to keep an egg from rolling. He takes out one of the eggs, strikes one end of it smartly on top of the table, and produces a small pool of yolk and white. The egg does not stand on end, as it should. It leaks. He leaves the other egg in the coffee can and begins to hunt for a percolator. This takes him back to the dark recess with the waffle iron and the other metal objects. There is no percolator, and he realizes why when he sees the Silex and remembers that the old-fashioned percolator is gone forever.

He knows he cannot work the Silex, so he gives up the idea of making coffee and thinks of opening a can of peaches. Before he can find a can of peaches, he has placed seventeen cans of other things on the floor. Now comes the problem of opening the peaches, and he goes through the drawers looking for a can opener. He can't find one and remembers vaguely having heard something about an electric can opener. He looks around the walls and spots the Mixmaster, but something keeps him from trying to open the can of peaches by putting it in the Mixmaster and starting the thing. He is suddenly no longer hungry.

The project of cooking something is completely abandoned, for he is faced with a much more urgent task: how to get rid of the mess he has created with the egg, and prevent his wife from finding out about it when she comes home. He tries to pick up the spattered egg, with no success, so he looks around for a cloth, and spots one neatly folded over the back of a kitchen chair. On this he wipes his eggy hands and, as the cloth falls open, he sees that what he has hold of is an apron. Panic seizes him now, and he wipes up the broken egg with the apron. This doesn't seem to work too well, so he gets water in a glass and pours it on the table top and then wipes some more.

The dilemma now is what to do with the apron. Many a husband, living in the country, would get the spade and bury the apron outdoors, but John is at heart a city man. The wild idea crosses his mind that he can hide it in the garbage can, but a misty sense of the fitness of things restrains his hand. He hurries into

the living room and stuffs the apron in the wastebas-
ket, but even as he does so, the dreadful compulsion
is forming at the back of his mind to wash out the evidence of his guilt. He takes the apron from the waste-
basket, goes upstairs, runs a tub of hot water, and
douses the apron.

What he has now is something so wet that it cannot possibly be dried before his wife gets home. Every
husband must work out this quandary in his own way.
The more timid men may try to hide the wet apron
inside an overcoat hanging in a closet, or under the
clean pajamas in a bureau drawer. The bolder ones,
like me, will spread the thing over a radiator, or pin
it to the shower curtain.

My own experience has taught me that nothing can
be successfully hidden from a woman, unless she hides
it from herself. The common housewife knows the
whereabouts of everything small, but she has a tendency to mislay waffle irons and the like, and the one
you found in that dark recess may cheer her up so
that she will forgive the incident of the apron. I would
get those seventeen cans off the floor, though, and take
that egg out of the coffee and put it back in the refrigerator.

CHAPTER NINE

File and Forget

I WANT to thank my secretary, Miss Ellen Bagley, for putting the following letters in order. I was not up to the task myself, for reasons that will, I think, become clear to the reader.   J. T.

WEST CORNWALL, CONN.
NOVEMBER 2, 1949

Miss Alma Winege,
The Charteriss Publishing Co.,
132 East What Street,
New York, N.Y.
DEAR MISS WINEGE:
    Your letter of October 25th, which you sent to me in care of The Homestead, Hot Springs, Ark., has been forwarded to my home in West Cornwall, Conn., by The Homestead, Hot Springs, Va. As you

know, Mrs. Thurber and I sometimes visit this Virginia resort, but we haven't been there for more than a year. Your company, in the great tradition of publishers, has sent so many letters to me at Hot Springs, Ark., that the postmaster there has simply taken to sending them on to the right address, or what would be the right address if I were there. I explained to Mr. Cluffman, and also to Miss Lexy, when I last called at your offices, that all mail was to be sent to me at West Cornwall until further notice. If and when I go to The Homestead, I will let you know in advance. Meanwhile, I suggest that you remove from your files all addresses of mine except the West Cornwall one. Another publishing firm recently sent a letter to me at 65 West 11th Street, an address I vacated in the summer of 1930. It would not come as a surprise to me if your firm, or some other publishers, wrote me in care of my mother at 568 Oak Street, Columbus, Ohio. I was thirteen years old when we lived there, back in 1908.

As for the contents of your letter of the 25th, I did not order thirty-six copies of Peggy Peckham's book, "Grandma Was a Nudist." I trust that you have not shipped these books to me in care of The Homestead, Hot Springs, Ark., or anywhere else.

Sincerely yours,

J. THURBER

P.S. Margaret Peckham, by the way, is not the

File and Forget

author of this book. She is the distinguished New York psychiatrist whose "The Implications of Nudism" was published a couple of years ago. She never calls herself Peggy.   J. T.

WEST CORNWALL, CONN.
NOVEMBER 3, 1949

Miss Alma Winege,
The Charteriss Publishing Co.,
132 East What Street,
New York, N.Y.

DEAR MISS WINEGE:

In this morning's mail I received a card from the Grand Central branch of the New York Post Office informing me that a package of books had been delivered to me at 410 East 57th Street. The branch office is holding the package for further postage, which runs to a considerable amount. I am enclosing the notification card, since these must be the thirty-six copies of "Grandma Was a Nudist." I have not lived at 410 East 57th Street since the fall of 1944. Please see to it that this address is removed from your files, along with The Homestead address.

Whoever ordered those books, if anyone actually did, probably wonders where they are.

Sincerely yours,
J. THURBER

Thurber Country

THE CHARTERISS PUBLISHING COMPANY
NEW YORK, N.Y.

November 5, 1949

Mr. James M. Thurber,
West Cornwall, Conn.
DEAR MR. THURBER:

I am dreadfully sorry about the mixup over Miss Peckham's book. We have been pretty much upset around here since the departure of Mr. Peterson and Mr. West, and several new girls came to us with the advent of Mr. Jordan. They have not yet got their "sea legs," I am afraid, but I still cannot understand from what file our shipping department got your address as 165 West 11th Street. I have removed the 57th Street address from the files and also the Arkansas address and I trust that we will not disturb your tranquillity further up there in Cornwall. It must be lovely this time of year in Virginia and I envy you and Mrs. Thurber. Have a lovely time at The Homestead.

Sincerely yours,
ALMA WINEGE

P.S. What you had to say about "Grandma" amused us all. A. W.

File and Forget

DEAR MR. THURBER:

I have decided to come right out with the little problem that was accidentally dumped in my lap yesterday. I hope you will forgive me for what happened, and perhaps you can suggest what I should do with the books. There are three dozen of them and, unfortunately, they arrived when my little son Donald was alone downstairs. By the time I found out about the books, he had torn off the wrappings and had built a cute little house out of them. I have placed them all on a shelf out of his reach while awaiting word as to where to send them. I presume I could ship them to you C.O.D. if I can get somebody to wrap them properly.

I heard from old Mrs. Winston next door that you and your family once lived here at 568 Oak Street. She remembers you and your brothers as cute little tykes who were very noisy and raised rabbits and guinea pigs. She says your mother was a wonderful cook. I am sorry about Donald opening the books and I hope you will forgive him.

Sincerely yours,
CLARA EDWARDS
(Mrs. J. C.)

Thurber Country

Mr. Leon Charteriss,
The Charteriss Publishing Co.,
132 East What Street,
New York, N.Y.
DEAR MR. CHARTERISS:

I am enclosing a letter from a Mrs. J. C. Edwards, of Columbus, Ohio, in the fervent hope that you will do something to stop this insane flux of books. I never ordered these books. I have not read "Grandma Was a Nudist." I do not intend to read it. I want something done to get these volumes off my trail and cut out of my consciousness.

I have written Miss Winege about the situation, but I am afraid to take it up with her again, because she might send them to me in care of the Department of Journalism at Ohio State University, where I was a student more than thirty years ago.

Sincerely yours,

J. THURBER

P.S. I never use my middle initial, but your firm seems to think it is "M." It is not.   J. T.

File and Forget

THE CHARTERISS PUBLISHING COMPANY
NEW YORK, N.Y.

NOVEMBER 23, 1949

Mr. James M. Thurber,
West Cornwall, Conn.

DEAR MR. THURBER:

Mr. Charteriss has flown to California on a business trip and will be gone for several weeks. His secretary has turned your letter of the 19th over to me. I have asked Mr. Cluffman to write to Miss Clara Edwards in Columbus and arrange for the reshipment of the thirty-six copies of "Grandma Was a Nudist."

I find, in consulting the records, that you have three times ordered copies of your own book, "Thurber's Ark," to be shipped to you at West Cornwall, at the usual discount rate of forty per cent. I take it that what you really wanted was thirty-six copies of your own book and they are being sent out to you today with our regrets for the discomfit we have caused you. I hope you will be a little patient with us during this so trying period of reorganization.

Cordially yours,
JEANNETTE GAINES
Stock Order Dept.

P.S. You will be happy to know that we have traced down the gentleman who ordered those copies of "Grandma."

Thurber Country

Mr. Henry Johnson,
The Charteriss Pub. Co.,
New York, N.Y.
DEAR HARRY:

Since the reorganization at Charteriss, I have the forlorn and depressing feeling that I no longer know anybody down there except you. I know that this immediate problem of mine is not in your field, but I turn to you as a last resource. What I want, or rather what I don't want, is simple enough, Harry. God knows it is simple.

I don't want any more copies of my book. I don't want any more copies of my book. I don't want any more copies of my book.

As ever,

JIM

P.S. It has just occurred to me that I haven't seen you for more than two years. Let's have a drink one of these days. I'll give you a ring the next time I'm in the city.   J. T.

File and Forget

THE CHARTERISS PUBLISHING COMPANY
NEW YORK, N.Y.

NOVEMBER 26, 1949

Mr. James Grover Thurber,
Cornwall, Conn.

DEAR JIM THURBER:

I haven't had the pleasure of meeting you since I had the great good luck to join forces with Charteriss, but I look forward to our meeting with a high heart. Please let me know the next time you are in the city, as I should like to wine and dine you and perhaps discuss the new book that I feel confident you have in you. If you don't want to talk shop, we can discuss the record of our mutual football team. You were at Northwestern some years ahead of my time, I believe, but I want you to know that they still talk about Jimmy Thurber out there.

Your letter to Harry Johnson has just come to my attention, and I regret to say that Harry is no longer with us. He went to Simon and Schuster in the summer of 1948. I want you to feel, however, that every single one of us here is your friend, willing and eager to drop everything to do your slightest bidding. All of us feel very deeply about your having turned against your book "Thurber's Ark." I note that in your present mood you have the feeling that you never want to see it again. Well, Jim, let me assure you that this is just a passing fancy, derived from a moment of depression. When you put in your last order for thirty-six copies, you must surely have had some definite use in mind for them, and I am banking on twenty years' experience in the book-publishing game when I take the liberty of sending these twenty books off to you today. There is one thing I am something of an expert at, if I do say so myself, and that is the understanding of the "creative spirit."

We have a new system here, which is to send our authors not ten free copies, as of old, but fifteen. Therefore, five of the thirty-six copies will reach you with our compliments. The proper deductions will be made on the record.

Don't forget our dinner date.

Cordially,

CLINT JORDAN

P.S. I approve of your decision to resume the use of your middle name. It gives a book dignity and flavor to use all three names. I think it was old Willa Cather who started the new trend, when she dropped the Seibert.   C. J.

THE CHARTERISS PUBLISHING COMPANY
NEW YORK, N.Y.

DECEMBER 13, 1949

DEAR THURBER:

Just back at the old desk after a trip to California and a visit with my mother, who is eighty-nine now but as chipper as ever. She would make a swell Profile. Ask me about her someday.

Need I say I was delighted to hear from the staff when I got back about your keen interest in "Grandma Was a Nudist"? The book has been moving beautifully and its ceiling has gone sky-high. We're planning a brief new advertising campaign and I'd be tickled pink if you would be good enough to bat out a blurb for us.

Yours,
LEON

THE CHARTERISS PUBLISHING COMPANY
NEW YORK, N.Y.
DECEMBER 15, 1949

Mr. James M. Thurber,
West Cornwall, Conn.
DEAR MR. THURBER:

I hope you will forgive me—indeed, all of us—for having inexcusably mislaid the address of the lady to whom the thirty-six copies of "Grandma Was a Nudist" were sent by mistake. I understand that we have already dispatched to you at your home another thirty-six volumes of that book.

My apologies again.

Sincerely yours,
H. F. CLUFFMAN

Thurber Country

WEST CORNWALL, CONN.
DECEMBER 19, 1949

Mr. H. F. Cluffman,
The Charteriss Publishing Co.,
132 East What Street,
New York, N.Y.
DEAR MR. CLUFFMAN:

The lady's name is Mrs. J. C. Edwards, and she lives at 568 Oak Street, Columbus, Ohio.

I have explained as clearly as I could in previous letters that I did not order thirty-six copies of "Grandma Was a Nudist." If you have actually shipped to me another thirty-six copies of this book, it will make a total of seventy-two copies, none of which I will pay for. The thirty-six copies of "Thurber's Ark" that Mr. Jordan has written me he intends to send to West Cornwall would bring up to one hundred and eight the total number of books that your firm, by a conspiracy of confusion unique even in the case of publishers, has mistakenly charged to my account. You may advise Mr. Jordan that I do not wish to receive the five free copies he mentioned in his letter.

If your entire staff of employees went back to *Leslie's Weekly*, where they belong, it would set my mind at rest.

Sincerely yours,
J. THURBER

File and Forget

P.S. I notice that you use only my middle initial, "M." Mr. Jordan and I—or was it Mr. Charteriss?—have decided to resume the use of the full name, which is Murfreesboro. J. T.

WEST CORNWALL, CONN.
DECEMBER 27, 1949

Mr. Leon Charteriss,
The Charteriss Publishing Co.,
132 East What Street,
New York, N.Y.
DEAR MR. CHARTERISS:

I am sure you will be sorry to learn that Mr. Thurber has had one of his spells as a result of the multiplication of books and misunderstanding that began with Miss Alma Winege's letter of October 25, 1949. Those of us around Mr. Thurber are greatly disturbed by the unfortunate circumstances that have caused him to give up writing, at least temporarily, just after he had resumed work following a long fallow period.

Thirty-six copies of Mr. Thurber's book and thirty-six copies of "Grandma Was a Nudist" have arrived at his home here, and he has asked me to advise you that he intends to burn all seventy-two. West Cornwall is scarcely the community for such a demonstration—he proposes to burn them in the middle of U.S. Highway No. 7—since the town regards with a certain suspicion any writer who has not won a Pulitzer Prize. I am enclosing copies of all the correspondence between your company and Mr. Thurber, in the hope that someone connected with your firm will read it with proper care and intelligence and straighten out this deplorable and inexcusable situation.

Mr. Thurber wishes me to tell you that he does not want to hear from any of you again.

Sincerely yours,
ELLEN BAGLEY
Secretary to Mr. Thurber

THE CHARTERISS PUBLISHING COMPANY
NEW YORK, N.Y.

DECEMBER 28, 1949

Mr. James Murfreesboro Thurber,
72 West,
Cornwall, Conn.
DEAR MR. THURBER:

I have at hand your letter of December 19th, the opening paragraph of which puzzles me. You send me the following name and address—Mrs. J. C. Edwards, 568 Oak Street, Columbus, Ohio—but it is not clear what use you wish me to make of this. I would greatly appreciate it if you would clear up this small matter for me.

Sincerely yours,
H. F. CLUFFMAN

P.S. *Leslie's Weekly* ceased publication many years ago. I could obtain the exact date if you so desire.

H. F. C.

File and Forget

THE CHARTERISS PUBLISHING COMPANY
NEW YORK, N.Y.

DECEMBER 29, 1949

Mr. James M. Thurber,
West Cornwall, Conn.
DEAR MR. THURBER:

You will be sorry to hear that Mr. Charteriss was taken suddenly ill with a virus infection. His doctor believes that he lost his immunity during his visit to the West Coast. He is now in the hospital, but his condition is not serious.

Since the departure of Miss Gaines, who was married last week, I have taken over the Stock Order Department for the time being. I did not take the liberty of reading your enclosures in the letter to Mr. Charteriss, but sent them directly to him at the hospital. I am sure that he will be greatly cheered up by them when he is well enough to read. Meanwhile, I want you to know that you can repose all confidence in the Stock Order Department to look after your needs, whatever they may be.

Sincerely yours,

GLADYS MACLEAN

P.S. I learned from Mr. Jordan that you were a friend of Willa Cather's. Exciting!

Thurber Country

Dear Jamie:

I don't understand the clipping from the Lakeville *Journal* Helen's mother sent me, about someone burning all those books of yours in the street. I never heard of such a thing, and don't understand how they could have taken the books without your knowing it, or what you were doing with so many copies of the novel about the naked grandmother. Imagine, at her age! She couldn't carry on like that in Columbus, let me tell you. Why, when I was a girl, you didn't dare walk with a man after sunset, unless he was your husband, and even then there was talk.

It's a good thing that state policeman came along in time to save most of the books from being completely ruined, and you must be thankful for the note Mr. Jordan put in one of the books, for the policeman would never have known who they belonged to if he hadn't found it.

A Mrs. Edwards phoned this morning and said that her son Donald collects your books and wants to send them to you—to be autographed, I suppose. Her son has dozens of your books and I told her you simply wouldn't have time to sign all of them, and she said she didn't care what you did with them. And then she said they weren't your books at all, and so I just hung up on her.

File and Forget

Be sure to bundle up when you go out.

With love,

MOTHER

P.S. This Mrs. Edwards says she lives at 568 Oak Street. I told her we used to live there and she said God knows she was aware of that. I don't know what she meant. I was afraid this little boy would send you all those books to sign and so I told his mother that you and Helen were at The Homestead, in Hot Springs. You don't suppose he would send them there, do you?

And here, gentle reader, I know you will be glad to leave all of us.

CHAPTER TEN

The Case Book of James Thurber

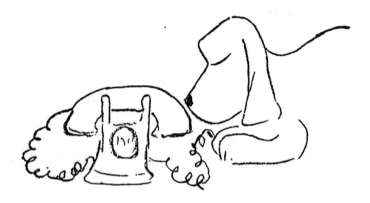

THE CASE OF the Gloucester Sympathizer was an easy one to crack, once I had sense enough to stop trying to crack it the hard way. I first heard about the Sympathizer one day last summer from a friend of mine at Annisquam, Massachusetts, near Gloucester. He told me he had called the Gloucester Telephone Company one day, to complain about something, and the operator had said, "One moment, please. I'll connect you with the Sympathizer." "She must have said 'supervisor,' " I said. This annoyed him, since he is proud of his ear and accuracy. "Not at all!" he snapped. "I said, 'Connect me with whom?' and she repeated, 'With the Sympathizer.' "

I wanted to know what the Sympathizer was like, when he was finally connected with her. "Did she begin by saying, 'Heavens to Betsy, isn't that too bad! I'm dreadfully sorry.' " He looked disappointed. "She was courteous, crisp, and competent," he said. I reached for my hypodermic needle. "Was she terribly solicitous?" I demanded. He frowned. "No," he said, "she wasn't."

When I got back to my home in Cornwall, Connecticut, I picked up the phone and asked the Cornwall telephone operator to connect me with the Sympathizer. "You're a caution, Mr. Thurber," she said, laughed, and hung up. Then I called the long distance operator in Torrington, fifteen miles way. She said there wasn't any Sympathizer in Torrington, but she was sorry it had happened, whatever it was. I could tell that she thought I was a caution, too. I was about to try Hartford, to see if there was a Sympathizer there, when it occurred to me to write the Gloucester Telephone Company and ask them about their Sympathizer. I got a prompt and cordial letter from the company, announcing that there wasn't any Sympathizer, and offering its consolations and best wishes. I got my violin out of its case and began sawing moodily in the general direction of "Chloe," lost in meditation. Naturally, I deduced at last, no reputable firm or corporation would employ a sympathizer, because the very existence of such a person would lend a note of gloom and insecurity to merchandising and other business transactions. I telephoned my friend and gave him the results of my findings in one sentence. "There isn't any Sympathizer," I told him. "Yes, there is," he snarled. "Go to hell," I said, and hung up.

The Case of the Gloucester Sympathizer was similar to the Case of the Young Woman Named Sherlock Holmes, a problem I solved the easy way a couple of years ago. George Spencer had told me that a guy he knew named Harry Huff was going to marry a girl named Sherlock Holmes. I said this was nonsense, because there isn't any girl named Sherlock Holmes. He said I didn't know anything about it. I said it was dangerous to believe everything one heard, and to go around repeating it. He snapped the leash back on his dog's collar, picked up its throwing stick, and went away.

I got out the phone book. There were two Henry Huffs listed, and I called the first one. "Nah," he said, "I'm living in sin with Dr. Watson. I thought everybody knew that." He was obviously the wrong Henry Huff, and I hung up on him. The second one turned out to be the right one. I asked him to spell out the name of his fiancée. Without hesitation, he said he didn't want to, so I mentioned George Spencer and what he had said about Sherlock Holmes. Huff was annoyed, but he finally told me the name of the girl he was going to marry, one Shirley Combs.

It reminded me of the Curious Adventure of the Oral Surgeons' Mouse, which had taken place thirty years ago when I was a reporter. The city editor answered the phone one day, and then sent for me. "The oral surgeons in convention here are about to operate on a mouse," he said. "Slide over and watch it." I went away and came right back. "What's the matter?" snarled the editor. "Wouldn't the mouse open wide?" "It wasn't a mouse," I snarled. "It was a mouth, it was a guy's mouth." This was a great blow to the editor, almost as great as that which befell the little boy in Pennsylvania Station who thought the announcer was announcing the Make Believe Train, only to find out it was just the old Maple Leaf Express, on its routine way again.

The Anatomy of Confusion is a large subject, and I have no intention of writing the standard treatise on it, but I offer to whoever does, the most singular of all my cases, the Case of the Cockeyed Spaniard. This remarkable piece of confusion took place in Columbus, Ohio, as long ago as 1922. I lived next door to a young couple named Dan and Janet Henderson at the time. Dan was a well-known reveler of the neighborhood, given to odd companions and peculiar pranks. One afternoon about six o'clock, Janet phoned me and asked me to come over. Her voice sounded wavy and troubled. "What's Dan up to now?" I asked. She sighed. "He's bringing home a cockeyed Spaniard," she said, "and I simply won't face them both alone." I slipped my brass knuckles into my pocket and went over to the Henderson house. "The only Spaniards I know of in Columbus," I told Janet, "are. a dozen students at Ohio State, but I doubt that they would be cockeyed as early as six o'clock."

It transpired that Dan Henderson had phoned his ominous message while Mrs. Henderson was in the bathtub. Their colored maid Mary had answered the phone. I interviewed Mary in the kitchen. She was pop-eyed and nervous. The physical stature of the Spaniard and the degree of his intoxication had obviously become magnified in her mind. "I ain't goin' to mess around with no cockeyed Spaniard," she told me flatly. "If he mislests me, I'll hit him with a bottle." While we waited for Dan and his friend to show up, I began to apply my special methods to the case, and before long I had figured it out. No doubt you have, too, since you are probably smarter than I was in 1922.

When Dan came home to his frantic wife, he was carrying the cockeyed Spaniard in his arms, but the fellow was, of course, neither cockeyed nor Spanish.

He was sad-eyed, four months old, sleepy, hungry, and definitely sober, as cute a cocker spaniel as you would ever want to see. Mary stubbornly clung to the name she had got over the phone, and her insistence on this pleasant distortion became generally known about town. People would call up the Henderson house and ask for her and say, "This is the Canine Census Bureau. What kind of dog do you have in your home?" Mary would always reply promptly and brightly, "He's a cockeyed Spaniard." I often wonder what ever became of her. I hope she is well and happy.

CHAPTER ELEVEN

The Case of Dimity Ann

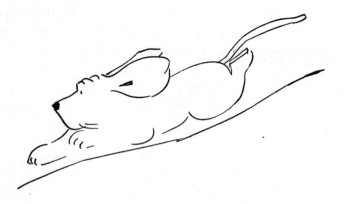

WHEN THE LAST guests left, after a party that had begun with early cocktails, proceeded gaily through wine at dinner, and then liqueurs and highballs, the Ridgeways stood in the open doorway of their house and watched the Bennetts' Buick flash its headlights at the turn of the driveway and disappear down the road.

"Let's have a nightcat," Ridgeway said. "I say

The Case of Dimity Ann

'cat' because nobody ever talked about cats the way Bennett talked about cats tonight. All I can think of is nightcat, hubcat, foolscat, freshman cat— I can't understand a cat man like that," he finished with a snarl.

Alice didn't like the snarl, which boded more Scotch, and she said, "I think I'll go to bed. It's after two," but she could see it wouldn't work. "I'll finish the one I have," she said quickly. "Then I'm going to bed." She hurriedly led the way back to the living room, as if she wanted to get the nightcap over with.

"Wives always tell their husbands where they're going," Ridgeway said sulkily. " 'I'm going to bed.' 'I'm going to put my foot down.' 'I'm going to tell you something.' 'I'm going crazy.' That puffball must have seventy-five cats."

Alice's highball glass, which was almost full, stood on the table by her chair. Mrs. Bennett had noticed when her hostess stopped drinking, with a kind of obvious quietness, twenty minutes before, and she had begun to remind Mr. Bennett of the hour, but the cat man was deep in a story about Alex, one of his Persians, and had to finish it. It seemed that Alex, who was as smart as a human being, could tell time, liked imported Chianti, and often made a certain music box play by lifting its lid with one paw. "Daintily, I suppose," Ridgeway had put in evilly, and when Bennett said, "I beg your pardon?" his wife had got to her feet. "Sorry you have to go," Ridgeway had told him, rising from his chair. "I was just reminded of a cat my first wife had, which I used to tie up." The women had intervened with a flurry of parting talk, and the Bennetts managed to get away without hearing about what Ridgeway had done to the first Mrs. Ridgeway's cat.

"You need some ice," Ridgeway said, and he got two lumps from the bucket on the bar and dropped them into Alice's glass. "I'll never forget Percy, one of my tomcats," he said mockingly. "He was smarter than a human being. He could whistle between his teeth, often winked, as God is my judge, and once, if my memory serves, killed a meter reader." He drank what had been left of his own highball and walked to the bar.

Knowing the significance of his various gaits, as well as the implications of his gestures and inflections late at night, Alice figured that if he had two more drinks, he would be up till dawn. "Not too heavy," she said. "It's almost three."

He poured a stiff drink, talking with his back turned. "Moriarty, another of my tomcats," he said, "could use an eyecup, and often *closed* the lid of the music box, thus putting a stop to 'Do Ye Ken John Whoozis?' What happened to that big slob in his infancy that made him cat-foolish the rest of his life?" He dropped into his chair, tugged at a lock of his

The Case of Dimity Ann

hair with his left hand, and ran his lower lip over the upper one. This usually meant that he was about to attack her old beaux, particularly one with the aggravating name of Rupert Llewellyn. Rupert had once sent Alice a volume of Emily Dickinson with the inscription: "This, when so much that is lovely has gone."

"What was it you did to Lydia's cat?" she asked hastily.

He clutched more hair in his left hand and gestured with his glass. " 'This, when all that was lovely is gone,' " he said in a jeering falsetto.

Alice twisted in her chair. "You've got it wrong," she said. "You always get it wrong."

He struck a match indolently, and slowly lighted a cigarette. "I don't care how it goes," he said. "I have no desire to be an authority on Rupert of the Lacy Touch. All I know is that a guy who writes 'This comma' is a lady cat."

Alice took a sip of her highball and said, "Well, speaking of cats, let's get it over with. What did you do to Lydia's?"

He took in and exhaled a deep breath, and was about to begin his story when Alice thought she heard something and exclaimed, "What was *that*?"

He glared at her. "I never started a story in my life," he said, "but what you heard something, or saw something, or remembered something. 'I just remembered something' has broken up more marriages than anything else." Alice took a larger swallow of her drink. "And don't keep saying, 'Get it over with.' What the hell kind of attention is that, anyway?" he demanded.

Alice gave him her cool smile and said, "I am all ears."

"THE CAT'S NAME was Dimity Ann," he began, "and I used to tie it up in the cord of my dressing gown to see how long it would take to get out. I never hurt the cat. The trouble was that I never told Lydia about it, and if I tied that cat up once, I tied it up a hundred times. I was going to tell Lydia about it," he went on. "I was going to say, 'Lydia, I keep tying the cat up all the time, if you want to know,' but I never did."

Alice sat forward in her chair. "Didn't you do anything about it?" she asked. "I mean didn't you talk to anybody?"

This puzzled and annoyed him. "Didn't I talk to anybody about what?" he demanded.

She smoothed her dress over one knee. "Well, it sounds like what they call a compulsion," she said. "Something you have to do, but you don't know why."

His annoyance grew, and his voice rose a little. "Whenever I do anything that I don't know why, I'll let you know," he said coldly. He seemed to become abruptly soberer, as he always did when he was caught between irritation and reminiscence. His eyes opened wider and looked clearer. "We haven't even come to the part that *you* would call compulsion," he said, "but *I* wouldn't. Anyway, it wasn't like deliberately running a lawnmower over a frog, or something like that—something your boy friend Rupert Valentino would do, and probably did."

"It wasn't Valentino," she said, "and you know it."

He finished his highball, and put the empty glass on the floor by his chair. "Llewellyn is worse," he said. "One day I was at the library and suddenly I stopped reading and went all the way home to tie up that damned cat. You've got to remember that the library was three miles from my house. I opened the front door and began calling, 'Here, pussy, pussy, pussy.' I knew Lydia wasn't home."

"I don't think I like this," Alice said. "I don't think I want to hear about it. I mean it sounds kind of deep-seated now."

He picked up his glass and rattled the ice in it. "I said, 'Here, kitty, kitty, kitty. Here, kitty, kitty, kitty,' but she was hiding. All right, all right, I found her and tied her up again, and then I went back to the library—after she got out, of course. When I came home that evening, Lydia said, 'The dotted-swiss cat has run away. I can't find her anywhere.'"

Thurber Country

"Is this supposed to be funny?" Alice asked. "Because it isn't."

He went to the bar with his glass again and she didn't say anything. She had several ways of not saying anything, and this was the one he disliked most. Even with his back turned, he could *feel* her not saying anything. "All right, all right," he said over his shoulder. "This is the drink that would kill Rupert, but I am not a thimble-belly. I am not the kind of man who loses one glove in a theatre and his wife has to look for it under the seats, either. And I do not extend my fingers when I examine my nails. I, by God, double my hand like a man." He made more noise than was necessary with the ice cubes and the seltzer bottle, and walked back to his chair with his lower lip protruding. Still Alice didn't say anything. He sat down and there was a ten-second silence, which he ended by saying, in his mocking tone, "Here, kitty, kitty, kitty, kitty, kitty, kitty, kitty, kitty, kitty."

She took another drink and said slowly, "Ah, shut up. I can't stand writers after it gets dark."

He looked deep into his highball and said, "The fastest time Dimity Ann ever made getting out of the cord was seventeen seconds. No fractions. You can put it down to research, if you want to. I am probably the only man in the world who knows the fastest time a cat can make getting out of the cord of a bathrobe. Seventeen seconds."

112

The Case of Dimity Ann

"What I would like to know," Alice said after a long pause, "is why you haven't told me this story before. I mean I wish you had, somehow. It's the kind of thing a man would tell a girl when he was going with her, I mean if it wasn't deep-seated."

He snarled, "I wish the hell you wouldn't keep using that damn word. You don't know what deep-seated means. It means worse than a bad cold, but you wouldn't know what that means. I didn't tell you about Dimity Ann because it isn't the kind of story a man thinks of telling a girl. It's really not important."

Alice jiggled the ice in her glass. "I don't like to hear you say it isn't important, because that's just the kind of thing that *is*," she said. "I mean if you think it isn't important, it probably is. But now you are trying to—trying to—what is it they call it when you don't want to face how important it is?"

He sat looking at her cloudily for a long moment. "You are the Goddamnedest fuzziest psychologist in the world," he said. "What you are buzzing around like a mosquito is 'overcompensation.' But, as usual, you are completely wrong. I am telling this story for the first time because this happens to be the first time I have ever had a great big lovable cat man in my house. I had not given Dimity Ann a single thought for eight years until tonight. Tonight all I had was cats—cats for cocktails, cats for dinner, and cats after dinner. Did I ever tell you about Rupert? He was one of my alley cats, and what distinguished him from the others was his ability to play a comb with tissue paper on it, and the fact that once he swallowed his own tail. This is what is known as psychological evasion."

Alice found, somewhat to her surprise, that she had finished her drink, and she held her empty glass out to him. He came over and got it and carried it to the bar. "Just a light one," she said. He made the drink and took it back to her. "Did you ever find Dimity Ann?" Alice asked. "I mean it would be awful if you drove that little kitten out into the streets and it died or something."

He laughed. "I forgot to tell you about that," he said. "Dimity Ann was picked up by Mary Pickford, who happened to be driving through in her limousine. The cat lived happily ever after, and became one of the greatest little pals Buddy Rogers ever had. This is known as minimization of the monstrous."

Alice turned her glass around slowly in her hands. "What makes me think you are trying to make me believe you are making this all up?" she asked. "I know you must actually have had a cat, or Lydia had one, because you could never make up the name Dimity Ann."

HE GOT UP and began to pace around the room. "This was a charming cat," he said, "but there just happened to be something between it and me, a kind of perverse communion. That day at the library, it was as if a faint, distant bell had rung. It was a signal from the cat to me. I think she actually wanted to be tied up, and the only thing that really worries me is that I was weak enough to give in to her. Lydia once had a Siamese cat that liked to have a Scotty drag it by its tail. The damn cat would lie on its back and wave its tail at the Scotty until the Scotty sighed and dragged it around. Its name was Asia. You won't believe this, but while the cat was being dragged, it purred."

"You just made that up," Alice told him. "You made it up to annoy George Bennett, and I think I know why you didn't tell him. You were trying to think of something that would shock him, but you decided that he would be amused, and you didn't want to amuse him. Now you are trying to make me believe you didn't tie up Dimity Ann, by telling obviously impossible stories." She looked at her wristwatch.

"I know," he said. "It's almost four, but I'll stay up all night if you insist on blaming me instead of Dimity Ann. It's always the cat's fault. They're strange creatures. You ought to know that."

Alice hadn't been listening. She sat forward slowly, frowning at the floor, and he knew that she was searching for a contradiction of something he had said. She found it, and looked up at him suddenly. "I wasn't buzzing around 'overcompensation,' " she said. "That's not the right word at all. Overcompensation is when you are nice to little girls and old ladies because you have been cruel to your mother. It means you ask for ice cream in a loud voice in a restaurant if you really think you are becoming an alcoholic. It means things like that."

He sat down, leaned far back in his chair, and studied her as if she were something in a museum. "What did you major in at college?" he asked. "If it was psychology—"

"I know what it is!" she cried. "I mean I know what it is when you pretend that tying up the cat wasn't important. It's defense mechanism." She brought this out triumphantly.

"You're getting colder and colder," he told her. "Defense mechanism, to use one of your cunning illustrations, is when a dowager at a formal dinner drops the ice cream down her bodice and then tells her hostess she is having a chill."

He began to drink his highball rapidly, and she said, "We're not going to sit up all night and argue, even if we do disagree on certain terms." He paid no attention to this and finished his drink. Then he put the glass slowly down on the floor by his chair. "I guess it *is* late," he said surprisingly, "and that goddam cat man wore me out. Like a fool, I just sat there and gave him my fixed grin and acted as if I were interested in his cats. The only one of them that had any guts was the one that could catch a baseball at thirty paces. It couldn't have been *his* cat. It must have belonged to the neighbors."

ALICE GOT UP and began emptying ashtrays and gathering up glasses, including his. She took the glasses out to the pantry, set them down, and stood there a moment frowning, going over the case of Dimity Ann. Suddenly she hurried back to the living room. There was something she had to tell her husband, and she was afraid he might have fallen asleep. When he did that late at night, it was almost impossible to bring him back to full consciousness. He was sitting in his chair with his eyes closed, but he was not asleep.

"The thing that worries me most is your going all the way home from the library to tie up the cat," she said. "If you had just happened to tie up the cat when you saw it, and were in your dressing gown, that wouldn't be anything at all. But I can just see you sitting there in the library and suddenly jumping up and forgetting where you were and tiptoeing out, to go back home, five miles."

He jumped to his feet. "I did *not* tiptoe," he said coldly, "and it was *not* five miles! I don't understand why you have to make it sound furtive. There wasn't anything furtive about it. It was as normal as tying a can to a dog's tail."

Thurber Country

Alice sat down and watched his gestures, which were wide and agitated, an invariable mannerism of his when he was holding an untenable position.

"Look!" he shouted. "When I got to the library I found out I had left my research notes at home, and I couldn't get anywhere without them. I went back to my house, as any sane man would, and in the course of hunting for them I tied up the cat. I have tried to tell you it was a little game we played together. Every time Ed Morrison goes home, for instance, he throws a few darts at his dart board. It was as simple as that." He sat down in his chair and began groping on the floor beside him for his glass.

"You have a wonderful memory," Alice reminded him. "You never forget anything, and you certainly wouldn't forget notes if you were going to the library to use them. I mean it wouldn't be like you." She stood up and walked toward the door into the hall, but stopped beside his chair. "Please don't rationalize this," she said quietly. "I don't want you to get in deeper than you already are."

"There is something serious the matter with you," he said crisply, in the tone of a trial lawyer cagily abandoning a shaky defense for a random attack. "You're trying to transfer some anxiety neurosis of yours to me by mixing me up in all this goddam terminology." He folded his arms and leaned back in his chair with the satisfied look of a counsellor who has brilliantly rested his case.

The Case of Dimity Ann

"What research were you doing that day at the library?" she asked.

He stared up at her. "How the hell should I know?" he demanded. "This was eight years ago."

She watched the left corner of his mouth turn up, the way it did when he was about to tell a daring story in mixed company or an inconsequential lie to her in private.

"I didn't go to the library at all that day," he said with a full grin. "I hid in a closet until Lydia had left the house, and then I came creeping out on all fours, calling, 'Kitty, kitty, kitty, kitty, kitty, kitty, kitty, kitty, kitty—' "

"Scat!" she cried loudly, as much to her own surprise as to his. Then she walked slowly out into the hall, and waited at the foot of the stairs for his last word. On nights like this, he always had the last word. She could see his right hand groping for his missing glass, and she could sense his mind and tongue searching for something final to say. She realized, after several long moments of silence, that he couldn't find the last word, for the simple reason that she had said it herself. She ran up the stairs as lightly and swiftly as a girl, restraining a new and unexpected impulse to clasp her hands above her head and wave them, in triumphant greeting to the invisible wives of all the writers in the world.

CHAPTER TWELVE

Look at That Darling Thing!

(WITH AN AIRY WAVE OF THE HAND TO THE LADIES
WHO CONDUCT THE SHOPPING COLUMNS IN THE RE-
SORT MAGAZINES I KEEP GETTING IN THE MAIL)

WELL, IT'S SUMMER AGAIN, and you might think
the shops would be going through a sleepy period, but actually they are all as awake and restless as
a burglar's wife. If a new trend is apparent, and I
think one is, it consists of household articles ingeniously designed to keep males, whether hosts or guests,
well in hand at parties during what are known as the
dog days. Mangrove & Shore, for example, have the
most divine cocktail tray to which half a dozen glasses
are cunningly but firmly secured by means of tiny nuts
and bolts. These come in both the cocktail and the

highball style, and there is one that has three of each. The glasses are filled with cocktails or highballs, or both, after the third round, and the tray is passed only to those gentlemen who are clearly on the point of starting trouble or "making something out of it." These cocktail trays can be kept hidden until the moment for their use arrives. The point is that the difficult host or guest will try to pick up a glass as before, only to discover that he can't get it off the tray. This gives the drinker the feeling that he has lost his mind or his strength, and is likely to sober him up for the rest of the evening. I can't promise that he will act any better the following day than he has since you married him.

This same shop also has other divine gadgets for the hostess, including a perfectly heavenly blackjack made of Spanish leather with a beautifully engraved silver handle. Phyllis Mangrove is glad to show the ladies how to use the blackjack without letting the guests find out what is going on. When the tipsy host sneaks out to the kitchen for a double whiskey and soda on the side, his wife simply steps from behind something and hits him back of the right ear. If she can't drag him into his bedroom by herself, the chances are that one of her women friends will be glad to help.

I ABSOLUTELY LOVED the tiny batteries and bulbs that can be concealed in a hostess's hair without being no-

Look at That Darling Thing!

ticed by her husband or her guests. If the undetachable cocktail glasses have not frightened the husband, the wife can accomplish the same effect by pressing a tiny button concealed in her left sleeve. This lights up her hair like a Christmas tree—the tiny bulbs come in red, yellow, green, and blue—and is calculated to scare the old boy so badly that he will behave the rest of the evening. When he cries, "Good God, Louise, your hair has lighted up!" his wife quickly snaps off the lights. The guests turn and stare at her and then at her husband, and two of his best friends can be counted on to take him up to bed, whether he wants to go or not. Mangrove & Shore also have stuffed owls and iguanas whose eyes can be made to light up, but I am afraid I wasn't listening too carefully when Grace Shore explained their use.

FOR UNWELCOME house guests the Inspiration Shop has just about the cutest discouragers and annoyances I have ever seen. These include inflammable ashtrays, a bathtub plug made of gelatin which looks exactly like the ordinary rubber plug, a charming assortment of cigarette boxes which you can't open—they are filled with cigarettes and are transparent—and a pair of bedroom slippers in which a mechanism has been cunningly concealed. The host or hostess should surreptitiously substitute these for the guest's own slippers. When he or she tries to put them on, they start moving across the floor. The guest is pretty sure to leave in the morning. If these devices do not work, the Inspirationers will show you the loveliest bath-room door you ever saw. It can't be locked or even closed, and is fine for the guest rooms of those who know the wrong kind of people. There is also a posi-tively wonderful bathtub which plays the national anthems of both England and America if the water reaches a height of more than five inches. This forces the bather to stand up, of course, and before long he will learn to use four inches, a great saving for hotels and guest houses whose patrons are inclined to be prodigal users of water in the dry seasons.

THE TOY SHOP, right next door, has just received a shipment of locomotives, fire engines, lorries, and other vehicles for the delight of Junior and Buster, and for the safeguarding of Daddy when he plays with the cunning youngsters on the floor and is so often caught off guard and knocked unconscious by one of the tots. To prevent this common accident, the new toys are made of rubber, a lovely soft but firm rub-ber which would not dent the skull of even the oldest father. For wives and mothers who don't give a damn what happens to Daddy any longer, the locomotives and the other toys also come in old-fashioned wrought iron.

Look at That Darling Thing!

THE FURNITURE SHOP had the strangest bad luck I think I have ever heard of, when it ordered seven daybeds and received from the manufacturer seven hundred sets of sleigh bells. This curious mistake was caused by the deafness of a woman secretary and by the fact that her marriage was approaching. She hears bells, but apparently does not like to think of beds, although who am I to go in for a Freudian analysis of this small untoward occurrence? Ben Dent, who runs the Furniture Shop, ingeniously decided to keep the sleigh bells, in spite of the fact that the Islands have never seen snow and have no sleighs and practically no horses left. He has made some terribly divine collars for cats, each collar containing four large bells, which can be heard a hundred yards away. This keeps the cats from creeping up on eagles and other large deaf birds. For husbands who hate to stay alone in remote houses at night and who lie awake all night thinking they hear something, Ben has constructed a sleigh bell harness for house dogs, since it is his firm belief that what the timorous husband hears is his own dog moving about in the yard. Mr. Dent did not want me to publish this fact on the ground that thieves would read about it, come into his shop, buy a sleigh bell harness and jingle it when breaking into houses. The husbands, Ben theorizes, would go back to sleep when they heard the sleigh bells downstairs, believing that it was their dog, and not a burglar who was opening the wall safe or stealing the silver. I think Ben Dent is positively silly.

Heavenly days, I've talked about just everything this time, and the Lord only knows what I will have to write about next month! Oh well, maybe there won't be a next month. You know how the world is.

CHAPTER THIRTEEN

Do You Want to Make Something Out of It?

(OR, IF YOU PUT AN "O" ON "UNDERSTO,"
YOU'LL RUIN MY "THUNDERSTORM")

I'M PROBABLY not the oldest word-game player in the country, and I know I'm not the ablest, but my friends will all testify that I'm the doggedest. (We'll come back to the word "doggedest" later on.) I sometimes keep on playing the game, all by myself, after it is over and I have gone to bed. On a recent night, tossing and spelling, I spent two hours hunting for another word besides "phlox" that has "hlo" in it. I finally found seven: "matchlock," "decathlon," "pentathlon," "hydrochloric," "chlorine," "chloroform," and "monthlong." There are more than a dozen

127

others, beginning with "phlo," but I had to look them up in the dictionary the next morning, and that doesn't count.

By "the game," I mean Superghosts, as some of us call it, a difficult variation of the familiar parlor game known as Ghosts. In Ghosts, as everybody knows, one of a group of sedentary players starts with a letter, and the spelling proceeds clockwise around the group until a player spells a word of more than three letters, thus becoming "a third of a ghost," or two-thirds, or a whole ghost. The game goes on until everyone but the winner has been eliminated. Superghosts differs from the old game in one small, tricky, and often exacerbating respect: The rules allow a player to *prefix* a letter to the word in progress, thus increasing the flexibility of the indoor sport. If "busines" comes to a player, he does not have to add the final "s"; he can put an "n" in front, and the player who has to add the "e" to "unbusinesslik" becomes part of a ghost. In a recent game in my league, a devious gentleman boldly stuck an "n" in front of "sobsiste," stoutly maintaining the validity of "unsobsisterlike," but he was shouted down. There is a lot of shouting in the game, especially when it is played late at night.

Starting words in the middle and spelling them in both directions lifts the pallid pastime of Ghosts out of the realm of children's parties and ladies' sewing circles and makes it a game to test the mettle of the

Do You Want to Make Something Out of It?

mature adult mind. As long ago as 1930, aficionados began to appear in New York parlors, and then the game waned, to be revived, in my circle, last year. The Superghost aficionado is a moody fellow, given to spelling to himself at table, not listening to his wife, and staring dully at his frightened children, wondering why he didn't detect, in yesterday's game, that "cklu" is the guts of "lacklustre," and priding himself on having stumped everybody with "nehe," the middle of "swineherd." In this last case, "bonehead" would have done, since we allow slang if it is in the dictionary, but "Stonehenge" is out, because we don't allow proper nouns. All compound and hyphenated words are privileged, even "jack-o'-lantern" and "love-in-a-mist," but the speller must indicate where a hyphen occurs.

Many people, who don't like word games and just want to sit around and drink and talk, hate Superghosts and wish it were in hell with Knock, Knock, Who's There? The game is also tough on bad spellers, poor visualizers, mediocre concentrators, ladies and gentlemen of small vocabulary, and those who are, to use a word presently popular with the younger drinking set, clobbered. I remember the night a bad speller, female, put an "m" on "ale," thinking, as she later confessed, that "salamander" is spelled with two "e"s. The next player could have gone to "alemb"—the word "alembic" turns up a lot—but he made it "alema" and was promptly challenged. (You can challenge a player if you think he is bluffing.) What the challenged player had in mind was "stalemate." The man who had challenged him got sore, because he hadn't thought of "stalemate," and went home. More than one game has ended in hard feelings, but I have never seen players come to blows, or friendships actually broken.

I SAID we would get back to "doggedest," and here we are. This word, if it is a word, caused a lot of trouble during one game, when a lady found "ogged" in her lap, refused to be bogged, dogged, fogged, jogged, or logged, and added an "e." She was challenged and lost, since Webster's unabridged dictionary is accepted as the final judge and authority, and while it gives "doggedly" and "doggedness," it doesn't give "doggedest." She could also have got out of "ogged" with an "r" in front, for "frogged" is a good word, and also what might be called a lady's word, but she stuck doggedly to "doggedest." Then there was the evening a dangerous and exasperating player named Bert Mitchell challenged somebody's "dogger." The challenged man had "doggerel" in mind, of course, but Mitchell said, in his irritating voice, "You have spelled a word. 'Dogger' is a word," and he flipped through the unabridged dictionary, which he reads for pleasure and always has on his lap during a game.

Do You Want to Make Something Out of It?

"Dogger" is indeed a word, and quite a word. Look it up yourself.

When I looked up "dogger" the other day, I decided to have a look at "dog," a word practically nobody ever looks up, because everybody is smugly confident that he knows what a dog is. Here, for your amazement, are some dogs other than the carnivorous mammal:

The hammer in a gunlock. Any of various devices, usually of simple design, for holding, gripping, or fastening something; as: **a** Any of various devices consisting essentially of a spike, rod, or bar of metal, as of iron, with a ring, hook, claw, lug, or the like, at the end, used for gripping, clutching, or holding something, as by driving or embedding it in the object, hooking it to the object, etc. See RAFT DOG, TOE DOG. **b** Specif., either of the hooks or claws of a pair of sling dogs. See CRAMPON. **c** An iron for holding wood in a fireplace; a firedog; an andiron. **d** In a lathe, a clamp for gripping the piece of work and for communicating motion to it from the faceplate. A *clamp dog* consists of two parts drawn together by screws. A *bent-tail dog* has an L-shaped projection that enters a slot in the faceplate for communicating motion. A *straight-tail dog* has a projecting part that engages with a stud fastened to or forming part of the faceplate. A *safety dog* is one equipped with safety setscrews. **e** Any of the jaws in a lathe chuck. **f** A pair of nippers or forceps. **g** A wheeled gripping device for drawing the fillet from which coin blanks are stamped through the opening at the head of the drawbench. **h** Any of a set of adjusting screws for the bed tool of a punching machine. **i** A grapple for clutching and raising a pile-driver monkey or a well-boring tool. **j** A stop or detent; a click or ratchet. **k** A drag for the wheel of a vehicle. **l** A steel block attached to a locking bar or tappet of an interlocking machine, by which locking between bars is accomplished. **m** A short, heavy, sharp-pointed, steel hook with a ring at one end. **n** A steel toothlike projection on a log carriage or on the endless chain that conveys logs into the saw-mill.

AND NOW, unless you have had enough, we will get back to Superghosts, through the clanging and clatter of all those dogs. The game has a major handicap, or perhaps I should call it blockage. A player rarely gets the chance to stick the others with a truly tough word, because someone is pretty sure to simplify the word under construction. Mitchell tells me that he always hopes he can get around to "ug-ug" or "ach-ach" on his way to "plug-ugly" and "stomach-ache." These words are hyphenated in my Webster's, for the old boy was a great hyphenator. (I like his definition of "plug-ugly": "A kind of city rowdy, ruffian, or disorderly tough;—a term said to have been originated by a gang of such in Baltimore.") In the case of "ug," the simplifiers usually go to "bug," trying to catch someone with "buggies," or they add an "l" and the

Do You Want to Make Something Out of It?

word ends in "ugliness." And "ach" often turns into "machinery," although it could go in half a dozen directions. Since the simplifiers dull the game by getting into easy words, the experts are fond of a variant that goes like this: Mitchell, for example, will call up a friend and say, "Get out of 'ightf' twenty ways." Well, I tossed in bed one night and got ten: "rightful," "frightful," "delightful," "nightfall," "lightfoot," "straightforward," "eightfold," "lightfingered," "tight-fisted," and "tight-fitting." The next day, I thought of "lightface," "right-footed," and "night-flowering," and came to a stop. "Right fielder" is neither compounded nor hyphenated by Webster, and I began to wonder about Mitchell's twenty "ightf"'s. I finally figured it out. The old devil was familiar with the ten or more fish and fowl and miscellaneous things that begin with "nightf."

It must have been about 1932 that an old player I know figured that nothing could be got out of "dke" except "handkerchief," and then, in a noisy game one night this year, he passed that combination on to the player at his left. This rascal immediately made it "dkee." He was challenged by the lady on *his* left and triumphantly announced that his word was "groundkeeper." It looked like an ingenious escape from "handkerchief," but old Webster let the fellow down. Webster accepts only "groundman" and "groundsman," thus implying that there is no such word as "groundkeeper."

MITCHELL THREW "abc" at me one night, and I couldn't get anything out of it and challenged him. "Dabchick," he said patronizingly, and added blandly, "It is the little grebe." Needless to say, it *is* the little grebe.

I went through a hundred permutations in bed that night without getting anything else out of "abc" except a word I made up, which is "grabcheck," one who quickly picks up a tab, a big spender, a generous fellow. I have invented quite a few other words, too, which I modestly bring to the attention of modern lexicographers, if there are any. I think of dictionary-makers as being rigidly conventional gentlemen who are the first to put the new aside. They probably won't even read my list of what I shall call bedwords, but I am going to set it down anyway. A young matron in Bermuda last spring told me to see what I could do with "sgra," and what I did with it occupied a whole weekend. Outside of "disgrace" and its variants, all I could find were "cross-grained" and "misgraff," which means to misgraft (obsolete). I found this last word while looking, in vain, for "misgrade" in the dictionary. Maybe you can think of something else, and I wish you luck. Here, then, in no special order, are my bedwords based on "sgra."

Do You Want to Make Something Out of It?

pussgrapple. A bickering, or minor disturbance; an argument or dispute among effeminate men. Also, less frequently, a physical struggle between, or among, women.

kissgranny. 1. A man who seeks the company of older women, especially older women with money; a designing fellow, a fortune hunter. 2. An overaffectionate old woman, a hugmoppet, a bunnytalker.

glassgrabber. 1. A woman who disapproves of, or interferes with, her husband's drinking; a kill-joy, a shush-laugh, a douselight. 2. A man who asks for another drink at a friend's house, or goes out and gets one in the kitchen.

blessgravy. A minister or cleric; the head of a family; one who says grace. Not to be confused with *praisegravy,* one who extols a woman's cooking, especially the cooking of a friend's wife; a gay fellow, a flirt, a seducer. *Colloq.,* a breakvow, a shrugholy.

cussgravy. A husband who complains of his wife's cooking, more especially a husband who complains of his wife's cooking in the presence of guests; an ill-tempered fellow, a curmudgeon. Also, sometimes, a peptic-ulcer case.

messgranter. An untidy housekeeper, a careless housewife. Said of a woman who admits, often proudly, that she has let herself go; a bragdowdy, a frumpess.

hissgrammar. An illiterate fellow, a user of slovenly

rhetoric, a father who disapproves of booklearning. Also, more rarely, one who lisps, a twisttongue.

chorusgrable. *Orig.* a young actress, overconfident of her ability and her future; a snippet, a flappertigibbet. *Deriv.* Betty Grable, an American movie actress.

pressgrape. One who presses grapes, a grape presser. Less commonly, a crunchberry.

pressgrain. 1. A man who tries to make whiskey in his own cellar; hence, a secret drinker, a hidebottle, a sneakslug. 2. One who presses grain in a grain presser. *Arch.*

dressgrader. A woman who stares another woman up and down, a starefrock; hence, a rude female, a hobbledehoyden.

fussgrape. 1. One who diets or toys with his food, a light eater, a person without appetite, a scornmuffin, a shuncabbage. 2. A man, usually American, who boasts of his knowledge of wines, a smugbottle.

bassgrave. 1. Cold-eyed, unemotional, stolid, troutsolemn. 2. The grave of a bass. *Obs.*

lassgraphic. Of, or pertaining to, the vivid description of females; as, the guest was so lassgraphic his host asked him to change the subject or get out. Also said of fathers of daughters, more rarely of mothers.

blissgray. Aged by marriage. Also, sometimes, discouraged by wedlock, or by the institution of marriage.

Do You Want to Make Something Out of It?

glassgrail. A large nocturnal moth. Not to be confused with *smackwindow,* the common June bug, or bangsash.

hossgrace. Innate or native dignity, similar to that of the thoroughbred hoss. *Southern U.S.*

bussgranite. Literally, a stonekisser; a man who persists in trying to win the favor or attention of cold, indifferent, or capricious women. Not to be confused with *snatchkiss,* a kitchen lover.

tossgravel. 1. A male human being who tosses gravel, usually at night, at the window of a female human being's bedroom, usually that of a young virgin; hence, a lover, a male sweetheart, and an eloper. 2. One who is suspected by the father of a daughter of planning an elopement with her, a grablass.

IF YOU SHOULD ever get into a game of Superghosts with Mitchell, by the way, don't pass "bugl" on to him, hoping to send him into "bugling." He will simply add an "o," making the group "buglo," which is five-sevenths of "bugloss." The word means "hawkweed," and you can see what Mitchell would do if you handed him "awkw," expecting to make him continue the spelling of "awkward." Tough guy, Mitchell. Tough game, Superghosts. You take it from here. I'm tired.

CHAPTER FOURTEEN

Take Her Up Tenderly

I HAVE A BONE to pick with the singing Andrews
Sisters, known to their many friends as the Girls.
A few years ago, with the assistance of a man named
Hughie Prince, they made up their own version of
"Sweet Molly Malone" and had it copyrighted. In
this arrangement, Molly does not die or even get sick.
The old ballad has long been in public domain, and
anybody can do what he wants with Molly, and almost
everybody has.

138

Take Her Up Tenderly

As every barroom quartet knows, the authentic Molly Malone died of a fever, or "faver," and no one could save her, and that was the end of Sweet Molly Malone. It is a well-known fact in Dublin's fair city, and everywhere else, that her ghost wheels her barrow through streets wide and narrow, crying, "Cockles and mussels alive, alive, O!" The Girls didn't want to sing it that way. I have it on the authority of someone close to them that they don't like anything to be sad or anybody to die. Their song ends like this: "So they both wheel a barrow, through streets wide and narrow, the man that she wed and Sweet Molly Malone." It depressed me terribly when I heard the Girls sing it that way over the air one windy evening in 1950.

That night I woke long before the infant morn was nigh and thought of Mary who went to call the cattle home across the Sands o' Dee and never came back, and of what a dose of Andrews' Ready Relief might do for her. I could see her returning safely home with the lowing herd ahead of her, and a mooing farmhand at her side. No longer would the boatmen hear her calling the cattle home across the Sands o' Dee in the sweet voice of that Death which Wallace Stevens has named the mother of Beauty. I fell to thinking of other dead and dying heroines, from Juliet to Clementine. "Beautiful Evelyn Hope," the Girls might sing of Tennyson's maiden dead at sixteen, "is getting better." I started to drop off to sleep again, but was jolted wide awake by three cheery voices distantly chanting, "I am mending, Egypt, mending."

I worry about what Mr. Prince and the Girls might do to Wordsworth's Lucy, if they ever set her to music. The case history of our heroine ends this way now:

> *She lived alone and few could know*
> *When Lucy ceased to be,*
> *But she is in her grave, and O,*
> *The difference to me.*

The saving of Lucy, I am afraid, might be managed like this:

> *She lived alone and few could know*
> *When Lucy married me,*
> *But we were wed in June, and O,*
> *The difference to me.*

Let me remind the Girls that two violets by a mossy stone are not twice as pretty as one, and that you simply cannot say, "Fair as a star when only two are shining in the sky."

I would not go so far as to prescribe death for all heroines. Sometimes it actually fails to touch the ladies with any discernible radiance at all, as in the case of Sweet Alice, whom Ben Bolt's friend remembers with such shocking clarity in the Thomas English verses. He recalls, as you know, that "She wept with delight when you gave her a smile and trembled with fear at your frown." Old Irv Cobb, in a fine monograph he wrote years ago about literary lunatics, pointed out that Alice's loud and mindless behavior when confronted by a simple smile or frown made her the greatest moron in poetry, worthy of a place a niche or so above the skipper immortalized in the line: " 'We are lost,' the captain shouted, as he staggered down the stairs." As I remember it, Cobb preferred the company of the crazy captain to that of the loony Alice, and I would go all the way with him if I could swim.

I don't know whatever became of the panicky captain, but Mr. English tells about the end of Alice in these lines:

> *In the old churchyard in the valley, Ben Bolt,*
> *In a corner obscure and alone,*
> *They have fitted a slab of the granite so gray*
> *And Alice lies under the stone.*

Alice's lonely end, alas, doesn't do anything for her, and the student of mythical heroines is forced to the conclusion that Death is sometimes only the stepmother of Beauty. There are those whom her cold kiss would disfigure. I am glad, for example, that neither Whittier nor Stonewall Jackson put a bullet through poor old Barbara Frietchie, and that the clapper on which Bessie was swinging at curfew time that day

CHAPTER FIFTEEN

The Girls in the Closet

I HAVE REACHED the age when the strangers I accidentally jostle on sidewalks say, "Sorry, Pop!" instead of "Watch it, Buster!" and the pretty young
women I used to help across the perilous streets now
snatch me from the path of ten-ton trucks, scold me as
if I were their grandpa on one of his bad days, and
hurry along with the throng, never giving me another
thought. This phenomenon of maturity, this coming
of frost and twilight to the autumn rose, would em-

143

bitter many men, but I take it in my totter. I have learned to embrace middle age, not to wrestle with it, and I accept the considerable difference between forever panting and being constantly short of breath.

The sedentary life imposed by advancing years often leads a man into his past. He sits around the house, going through old scrapbooks and photograph albums, catching glimpses of his younger self, trying to remember the names of the laughing girls in the 1930 snapshots, and arguing with his wife about lost afternoons and forgotten places. One evening, not long ago, with my shawl about my shoulders because of a nasty draught, I got out an album of pictures I had taken with my box Brownie nearly fifteen years ago in Southern France. I came across the strange,

FIGURE 1

The Girls in the Closet

obscure snapshot of the telephone shown in Figure 1, and it whisked me back to the Villa Tamisier, on the French Riviera, where my wife and I spent a tranquil winter before the second World War. I remember that remarkable telephone clearly, possibly because, as in the case of difficult women, I never did figure it out.

We had been in the Villa Tamisier nearly two months before I found out that there was a phone in the house. We didn't need a phone, because we didn't know anybody on the Riviera that season, except Olympy and Maria Sementzoff, who worked for us as gardener and cook. Then one night, about two in the morning, I heard a telephone ringing distantly and realized finally that it was somewhere in the villa itself. I stumbled down the stairs in the dark and followed the sound to the closed door of a small closet. Inside was the telephone, on the floor, snarled up in what appeared to be thirty feet of insulated wire. I took up the receiver and said, "Allo?" and a faraway despairing voice asked me in French if I were Monsieur Duronde in Bruxelles. I explained that he not only had the wrong man but the wrong country and hung up.

"What are you doing down there at this hour of the night?" my wife demanded from her bedroom. I told her I was trying to get a telephone off the floor. She came down, and we worked on the thing together, but the instrument was caught in an obstinate intestinal impaction and we had to leave it where it was. We lit cigarettes and studied the remarkable snarl of wire. My wife finally gave as plausible an explanation as any. She suggested that the owners of the villa, a doctor and his wife who lived in Nice, had probably carried the phone upstairs with them at night to save the cost of a bedroom extension.

"In the end," I put in, "the telephone was gradually imprisoned by the wires, the way an old rowboat is enveloped by morning-glories, and they couldn't get it loose."

My wife took it up from there. "Our landlord, the good doctor, is a fat man," she said, "and obviously couldn't reach the phone, so they had to move away and rent out their villa." I thought this over. "It isn't like the French to be driven from their homes by a lot of wire," I said. She thought *that* over. "Yes, it is," she said, and we went back to bed.

The next day I managed to get the thing loose, and was taking a time exposure of it with my camera when the ample and benign Maria came into the room. Nothing that I did ever surprised Maria. Once she had found me playing *boules* by myself—*boules*, as Maria well knew, is a game for two or more players.

On another occasion she came upon me tossing centimes at a small round hole in the center of an iron table on the terrace. She also discovered I labored under the childish delusion that the drawings I kept making could be sold for money.

Olympy and Maria must have spent a lot of time whispering in their quarters at night, trying to figure out the strange Americans. One day she asked me, "Are you paid to stay away from America?" That was the solution she and her husband had arrived at: *persona non grata* in the United States because of my peculiar personal habits, I had sought sanctuary among the tolerant people of France.

"You are photographing the telephone?" Maria asked, interested but not astonished. My French has never been much and my explanation of what I was up to must have sounded something like this: "I am with this telephone and my wife last night because a man has telephoned Bruxelles and we are thinking the doctor is not here because he was too fat to answer the phone." Maria never actually backed away from me, but her eyes in my presence became wary, as if she were watching a man juggling knives. "Is the telephone not extraordinary?" I asked her. She plainly thought I had taken leave of my senses. Since I couldn't think of the French words for wire or length or tangle, I was not able to support my own argument. My wife came downstairs to the rescue, but her French is competent only in dealing with problems of the kitchen, and the three of us merely complicated the situation.

"My husband thinks the doctor is taking the telephone upstairs," said Mrs. Thurber. From Maria's expression it was easy to see that she thought I had found the perfect mate. I lost my patience and began to shout in English, of which Maria understands only one word—"no." "What the hell was the phone doing on the floor in all that wire?" I demanded. "*Je vais chercher* Olympy," said Maria, cautiously, but my wife was determined to solve the situation in French on the spot, having just thought of the word for wire. The word for wire is *fil*, which happens to be very similar to the French word *fille*. So Mrs. Thurber, maintaining an air of tranquillity, said calmly to Maria in French, "There are too many girls in the closet." Maria left to get Olympy, but she didn't come back with him. I think he must have said to her, "Let us wait until they quiet down again. They have these spells, but mercifully they get over them."

Only a few days after the disturbing incident of the telephone, I drove to the movies in Cannes and parked my car on the wrong side of the street, not realizing my mistake until my wife and I came out of the theater. In Cannes, you are supposed to park on one side of the street on even-numbered days of the month, and on the other side on odd-numbered days. We were gratified, but surprised, to find that the windshield of the car had not been posted with an official police summons. I drove back to the Villa Tamisier, eight miles away, over a circuitous route that ended in a secluded nook behind the villa, a private parking lot by no means easy to find.

The next morning, while we were still congratulating ourselves on escaping a ticket, we went out to get into the car, and there, freshly pasted on the windshield, was the police summons with a black X beside "Parking on the even side of a street on an odd-numbered day." We stared at it silently and then my wife said, "*Je vais chercher* Maria."

Well, we got into another one of those three-cornered confusions. To Maria it seemed perfectly reasonable that our car should have been ticketed a day after the offense. Her analysis of the situation went something like this: "The police saw that yours was an American car and so they waited, perhaps in a doorway, and followed you home on motorcycles. It was necessary to find where you live and then to see whether you may not be diplomats or persons of great importance, who could not be arrested without involving the Cannes police and perhaps even the French government in a delicate embarrassment." She had to repeat this several times before we understood it. "How are they finding I am not important?" I asked her, coldly. This was easy for Maria. "They have records," she said, "and they telephone someone in Paris." Apparently it hadn't taken them too long to discover that a 1935 Ford sedan with the license number F-224 belonged to a person unlikely to involve the French government in a *cause célèbre*. I was smart enough to show up for my punishment at police headquarters at Cannes just after lunch the following day, and an amiable sergeant, redolent of wine and Brie, observing that we were innocents who did not know odd from even, or one day from another, let us off with a jolly rebuke and an exchange of compliments. "Ask him who they telephoned in Paris," my wife whispered. I took a stab at it, and the sergeant suddenly exploded into wide gestures and volubility. I think he was telling us how to get from Marseille to Saudi Arabia by ship. When he had finished, we exchanged deep bows, and my wife and I got in the car and started back for the Villa Tamisier. Neither of us said anything for nearly a mile, and then she spoke in her most authoritative tone. "They had run out of windshield stickers," she explained, "and had to go back to headquarters to get some new ones, and when they came back we had driven away."

"Then how did they know the license number of our car?" I demanded.

"They had written it down," said my wife firmly. I laughed at her innocence. "If they forgot to bring stickers," I told her patiently, "they would naturally have forgotten to bring the official notebook in which they write down the license numbers of—"

"Ah, shut up," said my wife.

CHAPTER SIXTEEN

A Final Note on Chanda Bell

(AFTER READING TWO OR THREE LITERARY MEMORIALS,
TO THIS OR THAT LAMENTED TALENT, WRITTEN BY
ONE CRITIC OR ANOTHER)

THERE WERE only three of us around Chanda Bell
at the end: Charles Vayne, her attorney; Hadley,
the butler (if he was a butler); and myself. The others
had departed with the beginning of the war, to new
dedications, or old hideouts, and the obituaries in the
journals after Miss Bell's death were erroneous in

claiming that the great, dark house in the East Sixties was, up to the very last, bedlam and carnival. Chanda Bell's famous largess and laissez-faire had, naturally enough, attracted the strange and the sublimated from the nooks and crannies of Greenwich Village. I had been particularly pleased to witness the going away of the middle-aged man who rode the tricycle, the schoolteacher who had resigned from the human race to become a bird, and Miss Menta, the disturbingly nude Chilean transcendentalist.

Charles Vayne, as regular and as futile as a clock in an empty house, showed up once a week with important documents that Chanda Bell would never sign. Some of them were dated as far back as 1924. A year of my friendship with the gifted lady had passed (so long ago!) before I could be sure that I knew what she was trying not to say, but Vayne never knew. Her use of the triple negative, in such expressions as "not unmeaningless," and her habit of starting sentences in the middle bewildered him, and so did her fondness for surrogate words with ambiguous meanings, like the words in dreams: "rupture" for "rapture," "centaur" for "sender," "pressure" for "pleasure," and "scorpio" for "scrofula." She enjoyed frustrating him, and she made the most of his discomfiture. "Praise me!" she would say as he handed her a fountain pen and the documents, which she always waved away. "Praise me!" she would command again. He invari-

A Final Note on Chanda Bell

ably reacted the same way. It had become a kind of ritual. "I repeat that I have not read a novel all the way through since 'The Crimson Sweater,' by Ralph Henry Barbour," he would say. His expostulations and his entreaties amused her for a while, but then she would poke at him with her cane and drive him off, crying, "He comes without armor who comes without art!"

Hadley, who ushered the attorney in and out every Wednesday afternoon, had one cold, impassive eye and one that he could cause to twinkle. It gave you the chill sense of being, at one and the same time, in the presence of advocate and adversary. His duties in the final months were sparse, consisting mainly of serving Madeira to Chanda Bell and me, or to Chanda Bell and Vayne and me, in the Gray Room, after four o'clock, when she had had her egg and had dressed and was ready to receive. One always stood in her presence, for it was Chanda Bell's conceit to believe that only the uncomfortable are capable of pure attention.

CHANDA BELL was fifty-seven when I first bent over her hand, and her mind seemed so keen and agile it was difficult to believe that she could confuse her guests, even her intimates, with one another. But she did. Charles Vayne was sometimes Lord Rudgate, an Englishman of dim background and cryptic reference, and sometimes Strephon ("a Jung mad I cussed in the Sprig"). I was alternately Dennis, a deceased painter, who had specialized in gun dogs for the calendars of coal companies, and one McKinnon or McKenyon, an advertising executive, who had attempted to deflower Miss Bell in a speeding motorboat during the panic of 1907. This was highly exasperating to such scholarly critics as Hudson van Horne and Dantes Woodrow, and they never came back after their separate agonized hours in the underwater gloom of the echoing Gray Room.

It is not congenial to me, at this time, to expose in detail how I became lost—if lost I became—in the "brilliant wilderness" of Chanda Bell's prose, or to reënact the process of equation, synthesis, and integration by means of which I was able to reveal the subtle affirmation compounded of the double negative of her unmeaning and her unmethod. This was ably— if mistakenly, still ably—set forth in my "A Note on Chanda Bell."[1] Upon its publication, she had sent for me, and in the fine years of intellectual intimacy that followed, my faith in her genius was more often reinforced than not. It wasn't until the last few months, when, by design or aberration, she began to discuss herself, between teatime and twilight, as if she were discussing someone else, that the blackest of a critic's ravens, uncertainty of his soundness, came to dwell in

[1] *The Neutral Review,* October, 1943.

A Final Note on Chanda Bell

my consciousness. It is a terrible thing not to be sure whether one has sought or been sought, not to be able to tell the hunter from the quarry, the sanctuary from the trap.

Chanda Bell had, in fact, commanded me to her salon, but had I not asked for it, had I not commanded the command, by the tribute of my unique and penetrating analysis of her work? She had cause to be grateful, and her summoning me to her side was, in my early opinion, the most natural of acts. Careless and churlish critics, in malice or mischief, had dismissed her bright and tangled intention with such expressions as "bloom and drool," "the amorphous richness of a thrown pie," "as dull as Daiquiris with the commodore of a yacht club," and "as far to the Right as a soupspoon." This last was the sheerest nonsense One might as reasonably have said that she was as far to the Left as a fish fork. The closest she ever came to mentioning politics was one day when, in a rare moment of merriment, she referred to Karl Marx as "Groucho." I myself had heard the faint and special obbligato of elfin horns in her work and the laughter in the dusty house, and I alone had seen the swift and single flashing of a naked nymph by moonlight.

IT IS HARD to mark the hour and day when the thunderhead of suspicion first stains the clear horizon of an old admiration, but I came to be drenched, in the horrid mental weather of last autumn, by the down-pour of a million doubts and dreads of Chanda Bell. I began to fear that she had perpetrated, in her half-dozen dense, tortured novels, one of the major literary hoaxes of our time, and to suspect that she had drawn me into the glittering web of a monstrous deceit, in order to destroy, by proxy and in effigy, the entire critical profession. We would sit in the Gray Room from four till dark—she had permitted me to sit, at last, with the compassionate concession of a queen—and she would pierce my thin armor of hope and prayer with sharp and studied flicks of her sardonic, allusive intelligence. "You have the scaffold touch of a brain certain," she told me one afternoon. This was in the best tradition of her infernal dialectic. I could figure, in accordance with her secret code, that I had the scalpel touch of a brain surgeon, or I could take her to mean, in perverted literalness, that I was doomed to die—and was about to—an awful death for my wrong and sinful certainties.

"You have found the figure, Thurber," she told me one afternoon, "but have you found the carpet?" This was accompanied by her shrewd, tiny smile. I could not determine whether she meant there was something to find that I had not found, or nothing to find at all, beneath the gleaming surface of her style. The devil of it was that I could not be sure of anything. I spent that night going over "The Huanted Yatch" with a

A Final Note on Chanda Bell

fine-tooth comb, searching for esoteric anagrams, feeling for what she had called "the carpet." I scrutinized, investigated, explored, took apart, and put back together again the entire fibre and fabric, uncertain of what shape and texture I was looking for. I read the thing backward, and I even tried to read it upside down and in the mirror of my bureau. I copied out one disturbing sentence and carried it about with me for close study: "Icing mellow moony on a postgate doves snow and love surrender." Its once perspicuous feel-meaning deserted me, and its cool loveliness became the chatter of a gibbon in my distraught consciousness. I could no longer tell whether it was beauty or balderdash. If it was balderdash, the book degenerated into the vivid cackling of a macaw, and my critique stood as a monument to a fatuous gullibility.

TOWARD THE END, Chanda Bell began to talk about herself in the third person, as if she were not there in the house but on her way to visit us. "I've asked her to tea," she would tell me, "but it will not astonish me if she fails to appear. Nobody has ever been able to pin her down." And she would study the effect of this upon me with her hooded gaze. She had lapsed into simple, declarative sentences, and this was a comfort, but I was deeply perturbed by the feeling that her outlandish fantasy and her revelations were new and planned inventions of her cruelty.

Thurber Country

"Chanda Bell," she said one evening, "had an allowance of two hundred dollars a week while she was still in pigtails. Her father, the millionaire industrialist, doted on the awkward, big-eyed little girl. He would bring her curtsying into the library for his cronies to admire. 'By God, she'll be the first woman president of Standard Oil!' he exclaimed one night. He had a stroke when he discovered that she proposed to become a writer. 'By God!' he roared. 'I would sooner see you operate an unsuccessful house of ill repute!' At fourteen, a dreadful thing occurred. The small son of one of her father's gardeners sold two poems to the *Atlantic Monthly,* entitled 'Ruffian Dusk' and 'The Strangler of Light.' Chanda offered him fifty dollars a week to write poems that she should sign and publish. The little boy coldly rejected the proposition, and his father, a stern Presbyterian, informed Chanda's father of the deal and how it had fallen through. 'By God!' the old man roared. 'At least she's not guilty of integrity, and that's more than I can say for any Bell in four generations except my grandfather and myself.'"

Miss Bell let her reminiscence trail off here, and she watched me from her divan with her penetrating eyes. "Ah," I said hopefully, "but she learned that day the high and holy importance of integrity, I trust." Chanda Bell gave me her sign of dismissal, a languid lift of her left hand. "You are the critic," she said. "I am but the chronicler. Leave me now. You perceive she is not coming." I rose and bowed. "Perhaps," I blurted out, "there is no Chanda Bell." But she had closed her eyes and turned away.

The next day, they took her to the hospital. "I have a panther near my hearth," she said, the first time they let me call on her. I went to see her twice again, the last time with Charles Vayne, who carried, with polished hopelessness, two bulging briefcases, which the nurse would not permit him to open. Chanda Bell was wandering in a far land, but she contrived a faint smile for each of her visitors. "Dear Rudgate," she whispered to Vayne, "what will become of meaning, thank God, when you are dead?" He tried in silence to make her grip a fountain pen, but she shook her head and turned to me. "Pretension has no plinth, Dennis," she said. "Ah, what a dusty answer . . ." Her voice and her heart failed, and the most remarkable woman I have ever known was dead.

THAT NIGHT, I called at her house, in the East Sixties. Hadley let me in. I had suspected him for a long time of being joined in dark conspiracy with Chanda Bell to make an end of me. I wondered, as I glared at the cold eye and then at the warm one, whether he might not be a frustrated writer, a bankrupt publisher, or an editor who had suffered a nervous breakdown. I jumped over the amenities of sorrow. "Her dying request," I said, "was that I should examine her papers."

The eyebrow over his twinkling eye lifted. "This evening, sir?" he asked.

"Take me to her desk and open it," I demanded.

There was a full second's pause, then "Certainly, sir," he said, and led the way into the Gray Room. "If I knew what you seek . . ." he began.

I turned on him. "I think you do!" I snapped. "I am looking for proof of whether I am an egregious ass or a uniquely perceptive individual. The line is sometimes thinly drawn between a tranquil old age in this city and exile, say, in Nassau." He seemed genuinely bewildered.

There was nothing in the desk except a large manila envelope, which bore my name on the cover. I tore it open with shaking hands. Inside was a single sheet of white typewriter paper on which there were three carefully drawn squares, one inside another. "What does it mean?" I asked. "What is it?"

"If you will permit me, sir," said Hadley, and he took the paper and studied it. "That, sir," he said, finally, "is what I should describe as a drawing of a plinth."

I seized him by the shoulder. "You *are* in on this!" I cried. "What does it mean? What's behind it? Who are you? What have you two devils been up to all these years? Why should you want to destroy *me*?"

A Final Note on Chanda Bell

He took a backward step and gaped. He was honestly frightened, or else he was a superb actor. There was no twinkle in his eye. "I do not understand, sir," he stammered, or seemed to stammer.

I let go of his shoulder. "My critical reputation is at stake," I said. "Has she ever written an explanation of her writing—perhaps to be sent to some journal or periodical after her death?"

Hadley appeared to frown. "That, sir, I could not say," he brought out.

I turned away from him and then whirled back. "What is the carpet?" I shouted.

He put several feet of the shiny floor between us. "I do not know what you mean," he said nervously.

"Would there be papers anywhere else?" I demanded.

He looked about the room. "Nowhere," he said hollowly.

I walked over and looked out a window for a long time.

Suddenly, Hadley began to speak. "She had promised to put me in one of her books," he said in a tone of sadness, or what came to my ears as a tone of sadness. Then his voice brightened. "I was to have been the uncharacter of the nonbutler," he said.

I came back from the window and glared at him.

"Her phrase, sir," he added hastily.

Thurber Country

I lighted a cigarette, inhaled the smoke, and blew it out slowly. "Didn't you appear in any of her novels?" I asked.

"Oh, but no, sir," he corrected me proudly. "I did not appear in *all* of them!"

It was as if Chanda Bell were in the room, her bright, dark eyes taking us both in with a look of veiled amusement. "It must have made you very happy indeed," I snarled. "Not to appear in any of her books was wonderful enough, but not to appear in *all* of them—the final accolade, Hadley, the final accolade." He acknowledged it with a grave bow. "What has become of her manuscripts and her letters?" I demanded.

Hadley put on a sad expression. "She burned them, sir," he said. "It was her last act in this house."

I looked for the last time at the Gray Room—the gray desk, the gray chair, the gray Hadley.

"Perhaps a glass of Madeira, Mr. Thurber?" asked the butler. I declined ungraciously and said that I must leave. At the door, with the welcome street so near and desirable, he coughed discreetly. "Do you wish to take this with you, sir?" It was the drawing of the plinth. I took it without a word. "If I may say so, sir," Hadley went on, "you were the closest of all of them."

I glared at him, but there was no twinkle. "How close?" I growled.

A Final Note on Chanda Bell

"Oh, very close, sir," he said. "Very close indeed." This time, I thought I detected the ghost of the twinkle, but I could not be sure. I could not be sure of anything.

IT HAS BEEN eight months since I found the plinth in Chanda Bell's desk. Nothing has happened, but I expect an editor to ring me up any day. "We've got a remarkable letter or manuscript here, apparently written by Chanda Bell," he will say. "Sent to us by her lawyer, in accordance with a request in her will. It isn't signed, but he says she wrote it, all right. Seems she never signed anything. Sort of laughter from beyond the grave, you might say. The old girl exposes her stuff as the merest junk. Proves her point, too. She takes a hell of a crack at your 'Note on Chanda Bell.' Thought you might want to read the thing and reply to it—we'll print you and her in the same issue. She calls the piece 'The Carpet,' for some reason. I'll shoot it along."

No such call has come as yet, but I keep a bag packed, ready at a moment's notice to fly to Zanzibar, or Mozambique, or East Liverpool, Ohio. Meanwhile, I have hit on a new approach to the works of Chanda Bell. I am trying to read them sideways.

CHAPTER SEVENTEEN

There's a Time for Flags

(NOTES OF A MAN WHO BOUGHT A CURIOUS CHRISTMAS GIFT)

D EC. 15—Yesterday morning at eleven o'clock I bought an American flag, five feet by three, and a white flagpole, eighteen feet high, surmounted by a bright golden ball, and now I am trying to figure out why. The incongruity of buying a flag and a flagpole in the middle of December as a Christmas present for my wife has begun to disturb me. True, the gesture is not so elaborate as that of the man in the madrigal who gave his true love a partridge in a pear tree, two turtledoves, and more than a hundred and twenty other gifts, counting the fifes of the eleven fifers and the drums and drumsticks of the twelve drummers, but it is approximately as hard to explain.

Thurber Country

When did the idea first come to me? Or was it merely an idea? Could it be that I was seized by the stern hand of Compulsion, that dark, unseasonable Urge that impels women to clean house in the middle of the night and men, or at least me, to buy flags in the dead of winter?

As I write this, twenty-four hours have gone by since I bought the large flag and the enormous pole, but unlike every other purchase I have ever made, including my banjo-mandolin and my Cadillac, the emblem and staff show no signs of dwindling to normal proportions in my consciousness. They occupy the whole landscape of my thought. Last night I woke up and thought about the eighteen-foot pole, realizing sharply the measure and magnitude of what I had done. I had bought, for the yard of my home, a flagstaff designed and intended for the grounds of an institution. Nothing smaller than a boys' school with an enrollment of four hundred would think of ordering a pole of that heroic height. A flag for a private residence is supposed to be hung out of an upper-story window on a five-foot pole. "Great God," I said aloud. "What is happening?" asked my wife, without waking up. It was a good question, a searching wind, a whisper and a rumor . . . a wink of the eye . . . a shake of the head . . . high as his house, they say . . . O say ain't you seen . . . every heart beats true . . . to the red, white, and blues in the night . . . where there's

There's a Time for Flags

never a post or flag . . . and forever impede Mayhew
Wade . . .

I became furled, at last, in sleep.

DEC. 16—I woke early this morning from a deep
dream of flags, and tried to remember when I first got
the idea, or when the Compulsion first got me. Did
it go back to the quiet years in Washington, D.C., at
the turn of the century, when I was fascinated by the
miniature flags that came with packs of Sweet Cap-
oral cigarettes? Have I always had a secret desire to
command a battleship, or own an office building, or
become headmaster of a boys' school with an enrollment of four hundred? Am I intent on blowing psychological taps over the memory of one of those hor-
rible captains of cadets at Ohio State University
thirty-five years ago? If so, why didn't I buy a bugle?
Oh, there must be some simpler explanation. Guilt.
That's it. That's what it is. Guilt, the most powerful
force in the life and psyche of the individual, more
durable than love, deeper than fear. But guilt about
what? What have I ever done that demands such a
vivid and magnificent symbol of regret? I can think
of nothing, except that, as a boy, I sympathized with
the cause of the Southern Confederacy and once announced, in Miss MacIlvain's Eighth Grade class at
Douglas School, that the South would have won the
war if Stonewall Jackson hadn't been killed at the
Battle of Chancellorsville. But this sin is surely not

black enough to call for so large a flag and so long a pole. I continue to ponder the provenance of the purchase.

DEC. 17—This is exactly what happened. I phoned Jack Howard about three o'clock on the afternoon of December 13th—was it only four days ago?—and asked him if he would go shopping with me. There was a Christmas present I wanted to buy for some-body—a flag. "A flag?" he asked. "You mean one of those clips?" "Not costume jewelry," I said. "If I were shopping for that, I'd take a woman with me. I want to buy an American flag. A big flag." "Oh?" Jack said, and, after a moment, "Sure. Fine. Fine. When do you want to go? I can't make it this after-noon." I arranged for him to pick me up the next morning at ten-thirty at my hotel in the West Forties. I had come to town three days before from my home in Cornwall, Connecticut, to buy a fl— to do my Christmas shopping.

When Jack and I were in a cab the next day, on our way to the famous Annin flag store, at Sixteenth Street and Fifth Avenue, he said, "They're worried about you at my office—well, not worried exactly, but inter-ested." I didn't say anything. "I told Chuck Nelson you were going to buy a flag and he said, 'What's he up to?'" Jack laughed. "All you need to do now," he went on, "is to buy a record of 'The Stars and Stripes Forever' and they'll have you up before the Un-Amer-

ican Activities Committee." He was right, and I was
frightened. "I wish you hadn't told everybody," I
said. "A thing like this can get all over town." I felt
that he was studying my right profile. "Well, what
are you up to?" he asked, with a laugh that didn't
seem genuine. "I'm not up to anything," I said coldly.
"I'm simply going to buy a flag. You don't have to go
with me if you don't want to." "Forget it," he said.
"I'll turn up my coat collar and pull down my hat.
You call me Joe and I'll call you Sam." I leaned back
in the cab, trying to indicate that I didn't want to talk
about it. He began to whistle George M. Cohan's
tribute to Old Glory.

Outside of the employees of the store, there was
only one other person in Annin's when we got there. I
realize suddenly as I write this that, in retracing my
steps, I have come upon the small and simple solution
of the case of the man who bought a flag in December.
For some years now I have not been able to see to get
around as well as I used to, especially in crowded
stores at Christmastime. I remember now a rough experience I had last year in a store filled with fragile
crystal and china objects, a store in which I had
bought Christmas presents over a period of years. The
last time I visited it, in December, 1948, I distinctly
overheard a clerk say, "Sweet God, here's that man
again!" I retreated from the store without buying
anything, and fortunately without breaking anything,

but the adventure had left its deep psychic mark. Subconsciously, since that day I had been seeking an easy, a less perilous, way out of my private shopping problems. My unconscious mind had found the answer. Hardly anyone would be shopping for a Christmas present in Annin's in December. I recall now that a line of verse, written by Clinch Calkins twenty years ago, had been running through my thoughts for months: "The peril streamed through us like flags." By an easy process of association, the peril of shopping had been linked up with the word "flags," and from there it was an even easier step for my mind to pick out the cathedral calm of the Annin store as the perfect place for me to buy my wife's principal Christmas present. The lady who stepped up to wait on us was gracious, competent, and unsuspicious. After all, you must run into all kinds of people in a flag store.

I see now that the flagpole was an afterthought. The five-by-three woollen flag that I decided on came to only five dollars, which didn't seem enough to pay for a gift. "How about a ten-by-six?" I asked the lady. "You don't want a ten-by-six flag," Jack said. "Not unless you own a skyscraper." It was then that the idea came to me of buying a pole, halyards and all, to go with the Star-Spangled Banner. "I would like to look at a flagpole," I said. "Certainly," said the lady, leading the way to the flagpoles. "Who is this present for?" Jack asked me. "Eisenhower?" "It's for my wife; it's for Helen," I said. I had hold of his left arm and I could feel him shrug, but he didn't say anything. There were flagpoles six feet tall, twelve feet tall, and on up. I finally selected an eighteen-foot pole, which came in three six-foot sections. The price, six times that of the flag, seemed to me suitable for a Christmas gift for one's wife. "What do you think of it?" I asked Jack. He sighed. "It's your life," he said. "Go ahead. Maybe an eighteen-foot flagpole is what Helen has always wanted." So I bought the flag and the pole and ordered them to be shipped to Cornwall, Connecticut. When we hailed a cab outside the store, Jack said, "Let's go somewhere and grab a drink." "It's only eleven o'clock," I told him. "Let's go somewhere and grab a drink," he said again, and we did.

DEC. 18. 11 A.M.—Now that I know, or think I know, why I bought the flag and the flagpole, I have begun to worry about the effect they will have on my wife. She is used to getting things from me no larger than a woman's hand. I hope the pole doesn't upset her too much, the way the father in Barrie's "Mary Rose" was upset when they told him his daughter had suddenly returned after twenty-five years in Fairyland. "I have been so occupied all my life with little things" was all that he could say. I don't want Helen to be stunned by a bolt from the red, wh— I mustn't go on like this.

2 P.M.—I finally told Ben Tuller, who does every-

thing about my place, from shooting crows to finding the coins I drop when I hang my trousers up, that I had bought a present for my wife that would probably arrive at the express office in four or five parts, three of them six feet long. "I can get a couple of my wife's brothers to help me get it over here," he said, "and maybe we can stow it in the garage till Christmas without Mrs. Thurber finding out, but I wouldn't count on it. Women have a way of knowing there are flags and flagpoles about. One thing I wanted to ask—" "How did you know it was a flag and a flagpole?" I cut in. He stared at me. "You told me yesterday," he said. Maybe I am losing my mind. I didn't remember telling him. "What do you want to know?" I asked. Before replying he gazed out the window for a moment, and then, "How do you aim to gift-wrap that pole?" he asked. I hadn't thought about that. I simply hadn't thought about it. And even if I could wrap the three six-foot sections, even if there was that much tissue paper and ribbon in the world, Helen wasn't strong enough to unwrap them. "I'll have to exchange it," I said. "Maybe they haven't shipped it yet. I'll exchange it for something else." "At *Annin's*?" asked Ben. "All you could get in place of it, I should think, would be a six-foot pole and maybe four more flags." I turned, without a word, and walked out of the room.

11:45 P.M.—I can't go on with it, I'm not getting anything done. I just sit here and make occasional notes. A few minutes ago my wife came into my room and said, "What are you up to?" There was that question again, that note of suspicion. "I'm planning to overthrow the government," I said. "By force, if necessary." "Then you'll need your rest," she said. "Come on to bed." As patriotic as she is, like all persons born in Nebraska, she'd be the first to lob a grenade into a congressman's living room, if I gave the word. She has what has been called "the strong loyalty of the wife." I'm going to bed now, but that doesn't mean I'll sleep.

DEC. 19—Well, the cat's out of the bag. This morning I got a letter from Annin & Co., and my wife, who always reads the mail to me, opened it and began to read it aloud. "No!" I cried, but it was too late. The fat was in the fire. The letter follows, in full, and will serve to authenticate these notes for such of my readers as may have suspected I didn't actually buy a flag and a flagpole but was just making it up:

DEAR SIR:

As per the request of our Miss Tal, we are pleased to inform you that the flag and the flagpole are already on their way to you.

We wish to advise you, however, that we have billed you for an additional $3.00, due to the fact that Miss Tal erroneously charged you for the pole without the 22-K Gold Leaf Copper Ball. This additional charge of $3.00 is for the Gold Leaf Copper Ball.

Miss Tal was of the thought and opinion that you

wanted the setup as displayed in the store, and the Ball is being shipped with the flag and the flagpole.

We trust that what we have done meets with your entire approval, and, hoping to be of further service to you, we are

Very truly yours,

ANNIN & CO.

GEORGE JAMIESON

I told my wife the whole story, beginning with my phone call to Jack Howard. She was wonderful about it. "I'm really glad to know what it is," she said. "Mr. Purvis, at the express office, phoned this morning before you were up and said he had two packages for you, one of them more than six feet long, and heavy. I've thought of everything, from a croquet set to a collapsible dog kennel." She considered a moment. "The pole isn't luminous at night, is it?" she asked. "I don't think so," I said, "but we could train a spotlight on the flag at night." "No, we couldn't," she said. "It's going to be evident enough the way it is, what with that twenty-two-carat gold ball." I began to breathe shallowly. "Three dollars seems pretty darn reasonable for a twenty-two-carat gold ball," I said. "Do you suppose they meant to say three hundred dollars?" My wife sighed. "Men shouldn't be allowed to shop alone," she said. "It's—it's dangerous." "No, it isn't," I protested. "Well, chaotic, then," she said. I settled for that.

There's a Time for Flags

Dec. 20—Last night my wife woke me up long after midnight. It turned out she hadn't been able to get the eighteen-foot pole out of her mind. She had been lying there thinking about a lot of other things, too. "I was just worrying about what the neighbors will think," she said. "I can't very well explain to them why you bought the flag and the pole, because it's too complicated. I understand it, but they wouldn't. They would just think you were facetious, or flippant, and you simply can't kid around about the American flag in a quiet, reserved New England community like this." I got up and lighted a cigarette. "I'm not kidding around," I said. "I love the flag. As garish as it is, it has beauty, dignity, and even grandeur, and that is something of a miracle." "For heaven's sake," she said, "don't tell people it's garish." "What has happened to the time of Man," I demanded, "when the possession of your country's flag is looked upon as subversive or something?" Helen sighed. "Well, anyway," she said, "we can't put it up in the snow. You'll have to wait till Flag Day. When is Flag Day?" "April 14th, I think," I told her. "No, it's in June," she said. "I'm sure it's in June, but it might be safer if we waited until the Fourth of July." "Maybe it would," I agreed. "Not even a senator could find fault with a man who flies the American flag on the Fourth." I got back in bed. Half an hour later I spoke to her in the dark. "I was just thinking," I said, "I

175

his genius at waggish confusion, and his light regard for the convenience of others. "Wait 'til you meet Zeph Leggin," an ecstatic neighbor said to me just after I came to Ludlow. "He'll drive you nuts, the old rascal, but you'll love him. We all do—except Miss Eldon. We always hire him for odd jobs. Used to be a master carpenter, they say, but now he doesn't give a good goddam. Funniest guy you ever heard talk, though. 'Lost my wife ten years ago,' he'll say to you. Play it straight. Say, 'That's too bad!' 'Yep,' he'll tell you, 'lost her in a drygoods store—I slipped out the back door.' Ha ha ha!"

For such bewildered foreign eyes as may fall upon these lines, I should perhaps explain that ours is a good-natured commonwealth of straight men and stooges, willing and eager to let a wall crumble, or a roof sag, or a pipe freeze if the vandal responsible for the trouble has a Will Rogers grin, a soft drawl, and a dry way of saying things. There must be something grave the matter with me. From the moment I set eyes on Ephraim J. (Zeph) Leggin, I wanted to poke him in the nose. For the sake of a fair record, I must report that Zeph took an instant dislike to me, too. Zeph was a-sittin' in front of his shack and a-playin' his mouth organ—he called it Ole Maria, I heard later—when Paul Morton, the neighbor I quoted earlier, led me up to him one afternoon. I was presented to Zeph Leggin. It was regarded as an honor, I had been told, if he stopped playing, opened his eyes, and deigned to speak. "Zeph, I want you to meet Mr. Thurber," said Paul. Zeph kept right on playing. "He's come to Ludlow to live—a new neighbor of ours," Paul went on. Zeph finished another bar of "Nellie Gray" and looked up—at Paul, not at me. "He a married man?" he asked. That nettled me. He hadn't acknowledged the introduction by so much as a nod, and I didn't like the practiced twinkle in his eye. I could see what was coming, and I beat him to the punch. It was small of me, I suppose, but I offer the purely human excuse that we had come to dislike each other in the first few seconds. "I lost my wife ten years ago," I heard myself saying in a strained, chill tone. The twinkle in Zeph's eyes died and a hard look took its place. With our rapiers crossed and clashing, we searched for each other's gullet. He was shrewd, all right, and not slow of mind. He knew that I must have been tipped off to this opening gambit of his. He threw a quick, baleful glance at Paul, who he must have figured was the tattletale. "Lost her in a drygoods store, eh?" Zeph asked me, and the Devil took hold of my tongue. "She died," I said coldly, and it almost brought Zeph up out of his tilted chair. Then he saw the astonished look that Paul gave me, and he knew I was trying to knock his foil from his hand by an inexcusable trick. "Now, that's too bad, Bub," he said nastily. "Come on, Jim, let's go,"

A Friend of the Earth

Zeph. "They's cockroaches." Miss Eldon's nose expressed disgust at the man's frank vulgarity. "Well, whatever they are," she said, "they're as big as mice." She had asked for it, she had walked right into it. Zeph's eyes twinkled and he put on his Sunday drawl. "The only way to get rid of cockroaches big as mice, Ma'am," he said, "is to stop drinkin'." She ordered him out of the house, and he shambled away playing "Polly Wolly Doodle" on his harmonica. "The man is gross," she told me. I had some difficulty maintaining an expression of grave disapproval of the gross man, but I managed it.

The grinning face of Zeph Leggin hung over my house in Ludlow like a moon. He didn't come around during the first couple of weeks, and I didn't send for him, although a number of chores needed doing, but his face was always rising in my consciousness, bland and bright and impudent, and I kept hearing the mischievous music of Ole Maria playing on the edges of my mind. The fellow had called me Bub and I don't get over such things easily. Somewhere, I felt, he was thinking up gags, or planning pranks to disconcert me. Paul Morton thought I was acting like a child about the town comic, especially when he found out that I couldn't use the studio behind the house until several rotted boards in the floor were replaced. "Why don't you get Zeph over to fix it?" Paul wanted to know. It was a foolish question and I gave him a foolish answer. "He insulted the memory of my dead wife," I said. Paul was amazed. "*You* started that," he said. "You spoiled his little joke about the dry-goods store, and got *me* in bad—he knew I had told you about it." "I'm sorry," I said, "but even if it hadn't happened, Leggin and I could never get along. Each of us wishes the other were dead. It takes all kinds of people to make up a world, Paul—the seasick sailor, the surgeon who faints at the sight of blood, and the Man Who Hated Leggin, as I am destined to be known after I'm gone. If Zeph were the last—" "Nuts," said Paul, and went away.

IT WAS ABOUT ten days later that I heard the sounds of someone moving around in the studio. I went out to investigate. It was Zeph. He was standing with his back to me, studying the rotted floor boards, and although he must have heard me come in, he didn't turn around. "Fella goes into this grocery store," he said over his shoulder, "and sez to the man, 'What you got in the shape of bananas?' 'Cucumbers,' sez the man." He tapped one of the boards with his shoe and turned around slowly. "What you got in the shape of tools?" he asked. I wasn't going to play any games with the old rascal. "I rented this house furnished," I told him, "and I haven't had time to find out where everything is. I thought you had tools of your own." He gave me the twinkle. "Won't know about that 'til

A Friend of the Earth

I get back home," he said. He took it for granted that the job of fixing the floor, like all other tasks of the kind, was his by inalienable right and I decided to let it go at that. "There ought to be a toolbox somewhere in the house," I said. He gave me the grin. "Twon't come to *us*," he told me. "We'll have to go to *it*." On the way out of the studio, Zeph stopped at a table and picked up a flashlight that lay on it. He clicked it several times and then said, "Needs new batteries. I'll be goin' by Barton's store in Danbury this afternoon. Want me to take it along?" I told him that would be fine and thanked him, and he put the flashlight in his pocket. I can't remember now where we found the saw, but the search lasted a good twenty minutes. Zeph examined it carefully and then put it down. "Can't use it," he said. "Left-handed saw." I studied it for a few moments. "I guess you'll have to bring your own, then," I said. He frowned. "Job a work comes a little higher iffen I furnish my own tools," he announced. I turned without saying anything and led the way out of the house. "When can you get at the job?" I asked him. He looked at the sky and then held out one hand, as if testing the quality of the air. "Bit dry for sawin'," he said finally, but he couldn't trap me into any comment on this. "There are some sound planks in one corner of the studio," I said. "Did you see them?" Zeph's grin crinkled the corners of his eyes. "I *saw* 'em," he said. We both turned away to see how he was getting along. I confess there was more to this than my instantaneous annoyance at the sight of the man. I was afraid of his tongue. He had thrown me over his shoulder, easily and in public. He was in the studio most of the afternoon, and if I had hoped that he would go away without dropping in on me, I was doomed, as the saying goes, to disappointment. Zeph never knocked on anybody's door. He just opened it and came in. He found me in the living room. "Job's done," he said. "So soon?" I snapped. He pulled the flashlight out of his pocket, walked over to my chair, and handed it to me. "Thanks," I said unamiably. "Send me a bill for the carpentry." "Got it right here," said Zeph, and he handed me a slip of paper. I glanced at it, and it seemed reasonable enough. Then I clicked the flashlight. It didn't work. "It doesn't work," I told him. He twinkled and grinned. "Needs new battries," he said. I should have known better. I should have said nothing. But once again I walked into his little trap. "You said you would take it to Barton's and have it fixed," I told him. His eyes crinkled. "Nope," he said. "Told you I was goin' by, didn't say nothin' about stoppin' in." That was too much for me. I brought the flashlight down with great force on the edge of a table and smashed it to bits. Then I turned slowly to Zeph Leggin, my eyebrows up, in feigned astonishment. "Defective," I said coldly. Zeph took his harmonica out of his pocket and rubbed it with the palm of his hand. He had lost the twinkle and the grin. It was a moment rare, perhaps unique, in the life of the great philosopher. Zeph Leggin couldn't think of anything to say. He walked out of the room playing "Nellie Gray," and that was the last time we ever spoke to each other. I got a man named Larkin, from Danbury, whenever anything around the house needed fixing.

I THINK it was in September that the Ludlow Men's Forum decided to ask Zeph Leggin to be the principal speaker at their monthly meeting. I saw the announcement in the Ludlow *Journal*. It said that Ephraim Leggin, Ludlow's most beloved citizen, had consented to address his neighbors and to share with them his rich and salty wisdom and his profound knowledge of life. The title of his talk, the *Journal* said, was "A Friend of the Earth." The Forum meetings were held in the small chapel across the street from the Congregational Church. There were about forty of us present when, after the reading of the minutes of the previous meeting and the reports of various chairmen of committees, the smiling Paul Morton stood up to introduce the speaker of the evening. It was an introduction dripping with marmalade and ornamented with flowers, and everybody loved it and everybody laughed and applauded as Zeph got slowly to his feet. I had seen him only once

A Friend of the Earth

or twice in passing since the incident of the shattered flashlight. I had felt ashamed about that show of temper and I hadn't even told my wife that I had broken the lamp deliberately. Zeph let his eyes roam about the room and they fell upon me at last, in a chair near the wall in a row at the back.

"Neighbors," began Zeph, "I ain't always bin like you good folks is nice enough to think, a man of philosophy and easygoing nature. They was a thing happened when I was a young fella that set me on the right path, you might say. My father give me a flashlight for Christmas one year and the battries wore out, like they is bound to do if a man aims to see more in this life than the good Lord wants him to. So I gave the flashlight to an uncle of mine, 'cause he sed he'd get it fixed for me. Well, he didn't *exactly* say he'd get it fixed for me. 'I'm a-goin' by Burke's store,' he sez, 'where they has battries. You want me to take it along?' So I sez that would be very kind of him. But he brung it back that evening and it wouldn't work when I clicked it. 'Needs new battries,' sez my uncle, and when I told him he promised to have it fixed, he sez, 'Never sed nuthin' 'bout havin' it fixed. Said I was goin' by Burke's store. Didn't say I was stoppin' in.' Well, sir, like many a man, young or old, that ain't growed up—and some of 'em never does—I lost my temper. I seen red and I smashed that there flashlight into a thousand pieces. I realized in a second this wasn't no way to act to a man a greater age and more common sense'n me, so I turned it off with a joke. I turns to my uncle and I sez, solemn-like, 'Defective,' I sez. Then—"

I got up quietly and quickly from my chair and started to slip out of the chapel. A number of the men turned and stared at me, and several frowned and said "Sh!" Bill Logan plucked me by the sleeve as I passed his chair. "Are you walking out on Zeph?" he whispered. I leaned down close to his ear. "Yes," I whispered. "Forever."

I had intended to spend the winter in Ludlow, but business took me back to the city, or, at least, I told Paul Morton and the others that business took me back to the city. My wife knew better, of course. She knew that Zeph Leggin was behind my determination to get out of Ludlow and stay out. Several months went by before I got up courage enough to tell her about the flashlight and Zeph Leggin's opening remarks on the night of the Forum meeting. To my surprise and delight, I discovered that I was able to laugh with her about what she called my straight-set defeat at the hands of the philosopher of Ludlow. She has promised, however, never to tell the Mortons about it, or Bill and Lucy Logan. I don't think I could stand that.

CHAPTER NINETEEN

The American Literary Scene

(AFTER READING SEVERAL ESSAYS, IN ENGLISH MAGA-
ZINES, ON THE PLIGHT OF THE AMERICAN WRITER
AND THE NATURE OF THE AMERICAN MALE)

I HAVE but now returned to England, and to my tranquil pen, after spending six interesting, rather, but scarcely restful weeks in America. It had been my purpose in setting out, or perhaps I should say my thought, to look at, but not exactly to examine,

189

in the journalistic sense of the word, what is going on
in the field, or fields—they are quite separate—of book
and magazine publishing over there. I bore, in my
portfolio, letters, pressed upon me by various friends,
to Mr. Horace-Lorimer, of the *Saturday Review
Post*; a Mr. Bok, whom my distinguished compatriot,
Lord Tweedley, had visited in Tamiami, long years
since, and who turned out unhappily to be deceased;
and to the strenuous Mr. William Rose, who in addition to writing for *New Yorker*, conducts a column
of chat about the underworld in the *New York Herald*, known for some amusing American reason as "the
Trib."

Mr. Rose was not in when I called at *New Yorker*,
a weekly journal of capricious opinion published,
with massive drollery, in an enormous hotel of the
same name, and I was unable, alas, to present my letter
to Mr. Horace-Lorimer, since I could not find him in
Boston, and, indeed, no one seemed to have heard
of him.

At this point, I am afflicted by the uneasy suspicion
that my American readers, if perchance I have any,
will condemn this small commentary for its confessed,
its flaunted lack of that kind of wearisome research of
which Americans, in their desperate and deplorable
love of fact, are so intensely avid. I have not
"checked," as they would say, a solitary statement
herein contained. I proudly, even gaily, protest that

at no time during my sojourn abroad did I descend to the vulgarity of "taking notes"—to use another Americanism. My prayer for forgiveness, if such I must seek, rises from the heart of a stout conviction that speculation, when cramped by certainties, is eased of its wonder and its warmth. So much, then, for apology.

New Yorker, the journal and hotel, rises, I should imagine, to a height of one thousand feet, and it contains somewhere between two and four thousand rooms, of which, I fancy, a third to a half is given over to the editorial offices. This amazing "plant" labours incessantly to turn out, on each Wednesday, a periodical that contains surely not more than twenty thousand words of letterpress.

One should not be led to assume that *New Yorker* is the most commodious plant in the city of New York. The American Broadcasting System, owned by Time-Holiday, Ltd., I believe someone said, is housed in Rockefeller's Plaza, a gigantic world of steel and granite, somewhat north of my hotel, that once accommodated the entire population of Kansas City. The ABS employs one hundred and fifty thousand persons, or perhaps a hundred thousand more than *New Yorker*. The Staff of that weekly is made up exclusively of wealthy residents of the city, curiously devoted to its prodigious commerce and shipping, its eccentric millionaires and their wives, and its several legends—the metropolis, of course, has no traditions.

It has several times been pointed out, I expect, that *New Yorker* letterpress sounds as if it were the work of one man. This comes delightfully close to being true. The letterpress is, in reality, written by three men: Mr. Alexander Wolcott, our own Mr. John Collier, and Mr. William Rose himself. Mr. Rose actually has two styles of writing, the exasperatingly lucid and understandable prose of *New Yorker*, in which one may never find comfort for even a moment in a weirdly managed construction or a charmingly uncorrected error of printing, and the sort of hard-hitting bully-boy mannerism he affects in his underworld gossip. On the side, it is interesting to note, Mr. Rose manufactures hundreds of kinds of tinned goods, which are marketed under the trade label of "White Rose."

I WAS appalled to learn, at a cocktail party (which degenerated, as not infrequently happens, into an alcoholic rout), that the Rose weekly, after employing America's most distinguished novelist, Truman Capote, had let him go, out of hand. My informant, a Mr. Busby or Bixby—it was infernally noisy at the party—told me that the magazine's controlling stock is held by a syndicate of Southern bankers, or bakers, who had conceived the fantastic notion that Mr. Truman's novel, "Other Rooms, Other Voices," was a deliberate assault on the virtue of Southern womanhood. He was given the sack, without ado or farewell, and New York publishers are now madly bidding against one another for the rights to his future work. This bidding is an odd and graceless procedure, in which the rival publishers outdo one another in wining and dining the prospective author. They are not above buying him expensive cars and other costly presents, and advance royalties in the amount of fifty thousand dollars are by no means unknown.

Publishers all occupy skyscraper penthouses, or "random houses," and although I was never actually in one of them, I can see them as clearly as if I had been. The publishers dictate ideas for novels to the writers, supplying them with titles and, in some instances, writing the books themselves. The American custom of seducing one's best friend's wife, and later killing oneself while on a "spree," out of fear that one is actually in love with one's best friend, is the basic theme most recently insisted upon by the publishers. It is good to be able to report that a small but sturdy group of male American writers (there has been no woman novelist since Miss Cather's death) stubbornly and courageously refuse to be enslaved or chivvied about. This little band consists of Ernest Hemingway, Elliott-Paul, the Dreiser brothers, Henry Miller, Faulkner, Upton Sinclair, Earl Stanley

Thurber Country

Gardner, and possibly a few others. The chances of this slender list being appreciably lengthened are far from good. A great many young American writers, having made sizable fortunes before the age of thirty, have retired, and pass their time drinking and attending the boxing matches.

Drinking, in the American literary set, has reached unbelievable heights, or depths, depending upon one's view. I think Spender, in his *Horizon* essay, went a bit far in intimating that many older authors have surrendered themselves completely to alcoholism. That word connotes, indeed it specifically defines, a form of almost incurable disease, whose most distinctive characteristic is the inability to stop, after one has started. I am sure that I got about as much as Spender, but it is obvious that he is able to sit up later than I am. Since all the American writers I met, of every age, were still carrying on at evening parties after I had left, it is impossible for me to estimate fairly how many of them eventually stopped and how many were unable to stop. I was informed that one American writer sat for seven days in an actors' club without going home, or ceasing his tippling, but this was told me by a gentleman well into his own fourth day and "unfolding" rapidly, and its credibility is perhaps negligible. It is safe to say that quantitative literary drinking in America is well beyond any and every mark that we English writers might fear, or hope, to achieve. American writers speak, quite openly and freely, of "drinking their luncheon" and of being "poured onto trains." The latest expressions for being intoxicated are "buzzed," "punch drunk," and "mugged."

The social intercourse of the American writer is realized, almost exclusively, in public houses or private homes and flats, between the hours of 5 P.M. and 4 A.M. the following day. When the writers meet in a public house, there is little conversation, the eleven hours of confined but distant intimacy being given over to a gambling game known as "matches." I think as much as forty thousand dollars may change hands in one night. The superficial observer might regard these nocturnal meetings as a sign of gregariousness, but they are, in reality, gloomily planned assemblages of separate lonelinesses. Friendship in America is indicated and proved by a steady flow of insult and contumely between friends, who smilingly accuse each other of insanity, depravity, spiritual damnation, duplicity, conspiracy, and the stealing of flowers from the graves of mothers.

Some American writers who have known each other for years have never met in the daytime or when both were sober. The coming together of writers in the home or flat of one of their number is invariably a signal for trouble to start. There is no discussion, to speak of, but controversy rages shortly after all are

seated in the living, or "rumpus," room. A controversy usually rises out of a fiercely stated prejudice,
hatred, or admiration by the host or one of his guests.
A novelist or essayist is likely to get to his feet, on his
twentieth or twenty-first highball, and announce that
he is "the greatest goddam writer in the world" or
that one of his friends is. This is instantly challenged
by one or more candidates for the special distinction
of greatest goddam writer in the world. The common-
est terms of opprobrium during these bitter debates
are: interior decorator, poet, chef, florist, and milli-
ner, since Americans believe that a talent in any of
these directions is *prima-facie* evidence of a lack of
virility, or at the very least a dearth of the true go-
getter spirit.

The foreign writer who is fortunate enough to be
present at one of those rare evening parties at which
there is discussion instead of argument is likely to be
at a loss, nonetheless, since the conversation holds
tenaciously to such highly specialized subjects as the
Buick, the Pontiac, the Cadillac, the Saint Louis Car-
dinals, the Cincinnati Communists, money, clothes,
 success, ladies of questionable discretion, and heels
(both goddam and round).

I had wished to make some small exploration of
Hollywood, home of the millionaire cinema writers,
whose life span is so shockingly brief. (I understand
that they are taken directly from the studio to the

cemetery, such is the pace even of death in California.) I must confess, however, that my farthest west in America was an hotel in the Eighth Avenue, a region of New York City charmingly named the Devil's Kitchen. The trip to this hotel marked the end of my American adventure. Others will follow me to those violent shores, just as, in the past, others have preceded me, from Mrs. Trollope to Geoffrey Gorer and Evelyn Waugh. The American writer will always be a richly rewarding subject for study.

He does not, to be sure, like to be studied, but he loves to be listened to, and thus the path of the foreign observer is made comparatively easy. It is well to remember that he resents all and every criticism of himself, his colleagues, or anything else, and he is likely to regard whatever you may say as "goddam patronizing." The American writer is constitutionally unable to "take it," but there is always the danger that he may turn on one, and "dish it up." In such event, it is advisable to apologize and to "powder out" before objects are thrown. Of course, if one has nothing to apologize for, one does not want meekly to "put up and shut up."

It is rather difficult, I see, to formulate a code of behaviour for the Englishman in America that is at once judicious and honourable. I shall continue to think about it.

CHAPTER TWENTY

Teacher's Pet

KELBY had not wanted to go to the Stevensons' for cocktails. It wasn't that he was tired out again, as his wife, Elizabeth, was always complaining. To prove this, he had, after making up his mind to go, insisted on walking, instead of driving, to the Stevensons' house, three blocks down and across the village green. He had wanted to have a quiet dinner at home, unpreceded by alcohol, and to retire to the library afterward and read du Noüy. Elizabeth would have at least three Martinis—he noticed, looking at her across the terrace at the side of the Stevensons' house, that she was already on her second—and that meant she might want to "go on" after dinner, or perhaps tear up dinner at home and drive to the Belleville Inn for more drinks and dinner there. She might even call up the Blakes from there and really get going.

"No, thanks," said Kelby as his host approached with the cocktail shaker; then, "Oh, all right, go ahead." And he held out his glass for his own second drink.

"Do you good," said Bob Stevenson, pouring. "Pep you up. You look a little gray—anything the matter?"

"No," said Kelby with the required smile. "No, not at all. I'm fine."

As a matter of fact, he was not fine. He had had, the day before, something very like a religious experience, of a darkly ominous nature. It had been brought on by his reading a magazine article dealing with the fears and neurotic disturbances of the human male in middle age. Kelby was three months past fifty, and the article had upset him, particularly in its reference to the sometimes disastrous shock caused by the aging man's recognition of the fact of death, the inevitability of his perhaps not too distant termination. Women, the article intimated, were better adjusted to the certainty of extinction and rarely gave it a conscious thought, but a man in his fifties or later—often earlier—might be stricken all of a sudden by the realization of impending death, with serious nervous or even mental sequelae.

Kelby had wondered, putting the magazine down, if the dread experience had come to him in his forties, say, and he had forgotten it. He chose to think that it had and that he had weathered it like the contemplative scholar he was. Upon arriving at this comforting decision, he had struck a match to light his pipe, and for no reason at all, since it was a sound match and no breeze was stirring in the library, it had gone out, as swift as a wink, as swift as death. Kelby had recognized the Moment. It seized him by the throat, and he found it difficult to breathe. His heart seemed to skip, and objects in the room began to recede. His pipe fell to the floor, and he held on to himself with a great effort, gripping the arms of his chair. There was sweat on his forehead and his wrists when he came out of his seizure. In a minute, he was his rational self again. It had been nothing more than a senseless panic induced by autosuggestion. He had actually managed a smile and a careless gesture of dismissal.

THE INCIDENT would not be dismissed so easily, it turned out. It set in train, as all Kelby's moments of weakness did, discomforting thoughts that took him back as far as his youth. It carried him relentlessly, against his will, to the awful day before the First World War when Zeke Leonard had faced him down, with a crowd of eager kids looking on and expecting a fight. Kelby marvelled that at fifty he still could not get that day out of his consciousness for very long.

The trouble had begun when Leonard, "a typical shot-putter," as Kelby, many years later, had described him to Elizabeth, started teasing him after school (they were in the eighth grade) by calling him "Willber, dear!" in a shrill falsetto, and repeating it at steady intervals all the way to the corner of Franklin Avenue and Pine Street. It was bad enough to be named Willber, with two "l"s, and to have his teacher call him by that silly name every day in class, but it had been unbearable when Miss Lemmert had called him "Willber, dear" one afternoon in the hearing of Zeke and several other kids as school was letting out. She had wanted Willber dear to post a letter for her, or to do some other small errand, a request that branded him at once a teacher's pet of the worst order. Willber Kelby was the smartest boy at Buchanan School, and from the third grade on his teachers had made no bones about it. Zeke Leonard, who had the brains of a pole vaulter, had hated Willber from the time they were seven for his intelligence, his name, his frail body, and his inability, according to Zeke, to do anything except study.

Kelby had turned on him that day, thirty-seven years before, but the grinning Zeke had pushed him, slapped him, bumped him, and kicked him around, holding one arm behind his back and calling attention to this handicap. Kelby had flailed his shorter arms a few times with ludicrous ineffectiveness, and then he had merely tried to cover his face against Zeke's pummelling. Finally, he had started to cry. The other boys had laughed and hooted and whistled. "Look—*both* hands behind me!" Zeke had sneered suddenly, and Willber Kelby had taken to flight, still crying.

"BREAK IT UP." The hearty voice of Bob Stevenson banged into Kelby's memories. "You having a conference with yourself? Here you go, Will."

"Thanks," said Kelby, holding his glass out for another Martini.

"Of course, I simply never get to know you, Mr. Kelby," babbled a woman, dropping into a chair next to his. "I've known Lizzie for simply ages, but you always seem to be *inside* yourself, as if you didn't want anyone to trespass on your thoughts. But here I am, a bold woman, determined to find out what you are thinking about, whether you want me to or not. Now, Mr. Kelby, what *are* you thinking about?"

Kelby fought off a frown and recrossed his legs. He was about to say something to the effect that he had been absorbed in the witty conversation going on about him, and then, perhaps because the gin had touched him, he came out flatly with the truth. "I was thinking about the time a boy named Zeke Leonard beat me up," he said. "I was a teacher's pet, and he beat me up."

"What in the world for?" exclaimed the woman. "What had you done?"

"A teacher's pet doesn't have to do anything,"

Kelby said. "It is the mere fact of his existence that makes the stupid and the strong want to beat him up. There is a type of man that wants to destroy the weaker, the more sensitive, the more intelligent." He must have let his gaze drift to his host, who was stirring up more Martinis.

"You mean the Bob Stevenson type?" the woman whispered into his ear in intimate understanding. Then, shifting back into high, "I know just what you mean. We have the *most* trouble with Elbert that way. He's so terribly sensitive. The older boys are always torturing him." She lowered her voice to a whisper again. "Young Bob Stevenson is the worst. He simply loves to badger Elbert. I do wish Elbert would stand up to him some day. It irritates my husband terribly that he won't take his own part. Do they get *over* it?"

Kelby's attention had wandered. "Once a fullback, always a fullback," he said.

"No, I mean the—well—teacher's pets," she explained. "You see, Elbert is really terribly smart—he's the brightest boy in his school. I wish *you* could talk to him, Mr. Kelby—it would do him a world of good. We are going to spend the winter here in Woodville, and he'll go into Junior High. It's terribly hard changing to a new school."

Kelby had been thinking while she ran on. Having finished his third drink, he was on the edge of his irritable phase, and the woman's babbling had not improved his mood. "I know Elbert," he said thinly. "He's like all the rest. They grow old, they die, and if they're lucky, they get buried. They do not change. The best that can be said for them is that they outlive the stupid and the strong. It isn't much, but it's something. They can snicker when they read the obituaries of the powerfully built. It is their only physical triumph."

"But they are not cowards," said the woman defensively, clipping the last word sharply. "At least, I know Elbert is not a coward."

Kelby had begun to twirl his glass by its stem. "There are a lot of comforting euphemisms," he said. "Hypersensitive, nonaggressive, peace-loving, introverted—take your choice."

The woman was beginning not to like the turn of the discussion. She had started to get up from her chair when from out of the house, letting the widely flung screen door bang behind him, came Robert Stevenson, Jr. He strode toward his mother, apparently oblivious of the guests. "Hey, Mom!" he said. "Geez, how's about some dinner—it's late."

Two of the guests arose at this broad hint, but Sally Stevenson waved them back to their chairs. "Sit down, sit down," she said. "It's early. We're not eating till seven-thirty."

"Geez, Mom!" said Bob.

"Speak to the guests, Robert," she commanded.

"You know everybody." He let a scowlish grin trail from chair to chair.

"Got a belly like a moose," said his father proudly, hovering above Kelby with the shaker. "Can't think of anything but the nose bag. Healthy, though, God knows. What did they bring you up on, Will—marsh-mallows?"

"Yes," said Kelby. "Toasted, mostly." Stevenson burst into loud laughter. Kelby, who had covered his empty glass with his hand, suddenly held it out.

"Good boy!" chortled Stevenson, filling it.

"Easy does it, Will!" called Elizabeth from across the terrace. The apparently amiable laugh that accompanied her warning fooled everybody except the other women and Kelby.

He raised his glass with a defiant look at his wife. "Here's to Junior," he said, "the greatest future full-back in the world!"

"Make it tackle," said the boy's father. "Bob wants to be a tackle."

"We never call him Junior," put in Bob's mother.

"You know that, Will," said Elizabeth.

"Tackle, then," said Kelby, and drank half his cocktail.

"Say, I almost forgot," began Bob Stevenson, Sr., and he proceeded to tell the terrace at large a noisy story about the predicament of a friend of his.

Kelby, not listening, studied young Bob, who had

dropped heavily but still gracefully onto the lawn and was moodily chewing a blade of grass and watching his father. The boy was thirteen, the same age Zeke Leonard had been in that faraway year of Kelby's humiliation. He was not unlike Leonard—big in the shoulders, long in the muscled arms, slender at the waist, restless, easy of movement and posture, and he had the same facile scowl and the sulky lower lip. Kelby hated his guts. He imagined that he was thirteen again, and he pictured himself squaring up to this big, ignorant boy. He spilled some of his drink as he indulged in the pleasurable fantasy of smacking Bob on the point of the jaw and sending him reeling backward to the ground. Kelby shook himself out of it with an effort. He finished his drink and stood up.

"How's about one for the village green?" asked Stevenson, who was an eager and watchful host.

"No, thanks," said Kelby. "Got some work to do tonight." He walked over to the only couple at the party that he liked and shook hands. He snapped a curt salute to the others and bowed to his hostess. Elizabeth could see that he was verging on his nasty state. She said goodbye to everyone hastily and joined him.

"Watch out for the marshmallows!" Stevenson called after him as they started around to the front of the house.

Elizabeth waited until they were out of earshot.

"What did he mean—watch out for the marshmallows?" she asked suspiciously.

Kelby shrugged. "Once a fullback, always a fullback," he said.

"But what did he *mean*?" she persisted.

Kelby turned on her. "He loves marshmallows!" he shouted. "He dotes on them, he's crazy about them. They are responsible for his wonderful physique and his mushy brain. Didn't you know that?"

Elizabeth took a dozen steps in silence; then, "I won't talk to you when you're like this," she said in the artificially calm tone he knew so well. She kept her promised silence until they had crossed the green. "I never saw Bob Stevenson eat a single marshmallow in my whole life," she announced.

Kelby wasn't listening. He was back in school again, on an afternoon before the First World War. As he got to the driveway of their house, he caught Zeke Leonard a staggering blow directly between the eyes.

Elizabeth noted that his right fist was doubled and she saw the hard glint in his eyes. "What *is* the matter with you?" she demanded.

"Nothing's the matter with me," said Kelby. "I feel fine. You want to call up the Blakes and go over to Belleville?"

"Certainly not," said Elizabeth. "We've got a lovely roast of lamb, and we're going to stay right

208

here. Besides, you'd be sure to get into one of your senseless arguments with Sam, and nobody would have any fun."

"We'll have another drink, then, before dinner," said Kelby. He could see her lips forming a firm protest. "I said we'd have another drink!" he almost shouted. She decided not to argue with him.

IT WAS ON SUNDAY, two days later, that Kelby, out for a walk, came upon young Bob Stevenson following Elbert truculently down Elm Street, increasing his cadence as his victim walked faster and faster. Elbert was almost at a dog-trot when he passed Kelby, who noticed that the boy's face was pale, and saw the hint of panic in his eyes.

"Hey, Ella!" Bob kept calling after the smaller boy.

Kelby was going to stop Bob and give him a sharp talking-to, and then something decided him to let the boy continue his pursuit. Bob passed Kelby without acknowledging that he saw him, calling "Hey, Ella!" in a mocking tone that had picked up an octave. Kelby turned around and followed the boys, but at a slower pace than theirs. Bob overhauled his quarry at the corner of Maple Street, and Kelby saw him reach out and whirl the smaller boy around. By the time Kelby came up to them, Bob, his back to the man, had flipped Elbert's cap off with a swift, insolent gesture. "You want to make anything out of it?" Bob was challenging. Elbert, panting, reached for his cap. "Leave it lay," said Bob, ruffling the boy's hair with his left hand. The future tackle stepped to where the cap lay and place-kicked it into the street. Then he strolled indolently toward the other boy, like a cop closing in on a traffic violator. He put out his hand slowly and took hold of Elbert's nose.

Kelby took two quick steps, grabbed Bob by the shoulder, and flung him around.

"Cut it out!" Bob said.

"Go on home!" snapped Kelby. "Go on!"

Bob scowled, and his lower lip stuck out. For three seconds, he tried to stare Kelby down; then he shrugged, made a noise with his lips, and started to saunter away.

"Wait a minute!" said Kelby harshly. Bob turned in surprise. "Pick up his cap and give it to him," said Kelby.

Bob glared. "Let him pick up his own cap," he said. "It ain't mine."

"Pick it up," yelled Kelby, "or, by God, I'll hold you over it by your ankles and make you pick it up with your teeth!"

Bob's eyebrows went up. He looked at Kelby's face and then away from it. He walked slowly to the cap in the street, spat neatly past it, and swept it up with his right hand. He tossed it at Elbert, who missed it.

Teacher's Pet

"So long, Ella," said Bob. "Keep your nose clean."
He moved off down the street, whistling.

Through this scene, Elbert had stood where he was
when the cap was knocked off his head. He was snif-
fling and whimpering. "Shut up!" shouted Kelby.
"Shut up!" But the boy kept on. Kelby looked at his
quivering lower lip and at the convulsion of his stomach. Elbert was fighting to gain control of himself, but
he lost the battle and began to weep unrestrainedly.
Kelby was suddenly upon him. He grabbed him
tightly by the shoulders and shook him until his head
bobbed back and forth. He let go of the boy's left
shoulder and slapped him on the cheek. "You little crybaby!" sobbed Kelby. "You goddam little
coward!"

Mr. Reynolds, who rounded the corner at that moment, had considerable difficulty pulling the grown
man off the little boy. "I've seen some bullies in my
time," Mr. Reynolds told the elder Stevenson later,
"but I never saw anything to match that." Robert Stevenson, Sr., slowly struck a match and slowly lighted
a cigarette. He put on his expression of profound wisdom, his lips tightening, his head slightly to one side.
"Young Bob tells me Kelby threatened *him*, too," he
said. He took in an enormous lungful of smoke and let
it out gradually, studying its pattern on the air. "You
never know about a man, Reynolds," he said. "You
just never know."

CHAPTER TWENTY-ONE

Shake Hands with
Birdey Doggett

JOHN BIRDEY DOGGETT, known as Birdey to the few people who speak to him, must be fifty-three now, but he wears his years with a smirk and he is as bad a practical joker as ever. Other American cutups in the grand tradition began to disappear in October, 1929, and they are as hard to find now as bison, but Doggett's waggishness has no calendar. You must have run into him at some party or other—he's the man whose right hand comes off when you try to shake it. The late George Bancroft once pulled that gag in a movie, but that was so long ago the picture must be a cherished item in the Museum of Modern Art's film library.

Even now, when everybody else was running the

gamut of bomb fear, from A to H, Birdey Doggett was at Grand Central with one roller-skate, which he managed to attach to the shoe of a man sleeping on a bench. When the fellow woke and stood up, he described a brief, desperate semicircle, clutched a woman shopper about the knees, dragged her and her bundles to the cold floor, and was attacked by her muzzled Scotty. Doggett, as always, was the first to lend a hand, helping the woman to her feet and then turning to the man. "Where the hell's your other skate?" he demanded sharply. "That's what's caused all this trouble." He took his skate off the victim's foot and disappeared into the crowd that had begun to gather. "What's the matter over there?" a small man asked him apprehensively. Doggett shrugged. "Oh, they found a woman with a ticking package," he said. The other man turned and left the station, missing the train he had told his wife he would take. Doggett's pranks usually have the effect of involving people on their far edges, one or two of whom have been divorced as a result.

A publisher I know thinks Doggett would make a good story. I disagree, because I don't think there's anything good about the fellow, but I have done some checking up on him out of force of habit. His father, the late Carrol Lamb Doggett, was a Methodist minister and his mother was a witch, born Etta June Birdey. When her son was only ten she taught him how to set strangers' umbrellas on fire. After an April shower she would sally forth with the little hellion—they lived in Dayton—in search of a citizen with a floppy umbrella. After an April shower, Dayton men lower their umbrellas without bothering to roll them. Mrs. Doggett would hunt until she found a man waiting for a streetcar, his umbrella sagging open at his side. She would then surreptitiously fill the umbrella with paper, several dozen kitchen matches, and perhaps one or two pingpong balls. As the streetcar approached she would drop a lighted match into the umbrella. Now, Hell hath no dismay like that of a gentleman whose wet umbrella suddenly bursts into flame. Instead of rolling the thing to smother the blaze, or simply throwing it away, nine out of ten men, according to Doggett's statistics, will flail it around in the air, thus increasing the conflagration. Many of Mrs. Doggett's victims were arrested for disturbing the peace or for arson.

Birdey Doggett has never been much interested in the exasperating paraphernalia of the trick and puzzle shops. Oh, he still uses the wax hand, and he has tried out dribble glasses, whoopee cushions, the foul smelling stuff you put on chair bottoms to make people think they have sat on a lighted cigarette, and other such juvenile props, but they never got a real hold on his fancy. He likes the elaborate rib involving a lot of people, the more the better. He will take a

sackful of cold poached eggs to some crowded Fifth
Avenue store at Christmas time and slip them, one at
a time, into the pockets of shoppers' husbands, and he
dreams of bumping into a woman visitor in the Ancient Glass and Crystal Room of some museum, dropping an ordinary table tumbler on the tile floor, sob-
bing, "Sweet God, lady, you have broken the sacred
chalice of King Alexander!" and making her believe
it. He has pulled this gag over and over since 1924, but
never successfully, with the result that he has appeared sixteen times in Jefferson Market Court alone
on charges of disturbing the peace, jostling, and attempted rape.

What Doggett probably enjoys more than anything
else is following a couple of women along Fifth Avenue or Madison, keeping discreetly out of sight, but
well within earshot, until he hears one of the two
ladies call the other by name. He says that women are
fond of using each other's full name, as in "Why,
Miriam Shertle, I never heard of such a thing in all
my born days!" As soon as Miss Shertle, let us say, has
been thus fully identified, Doggett will walk briskly
ahead for several blocks, and then retrace his steps.
This soon brings him face to face with his quarry,
upon whom he will pounce with a delighted, "Why,
Miriam Shertle, fancy meeting you here! Uncross
those lovely eyes, and tell me how you've been!" A
young woman he once accosted like this in Harris-

burg asked him to her house for cocktails, in the hope that some member of her family would know who he was, but nobody was home. His hostess turned out to be a bore, so Birdey put knockout drops in her second martini, and after she had passed out, he stole a marble plaque of Kitchener from her mother's room and went away. The next day it arrived at the Shertle's, beautifully wrapped and bearing a card with the simple legend: "Merry Christmas from the President of the United States."

John Birdey Doggett married a tapioca brain one afternoon twenty years ago, possibly because he had lost a bet. Nobody knows. He took her to his house and told her to wait in the living room while he went upstairs and quieted his two Great Danes. He put a record of a dogfight on a phonograph he kept in his bedroom and slipped quietly out the back door. At three in the morning, he showed up in the living room with two match players, Lew Getling and Vic Talbot.

"Who is this disconsolate female," Talbot demanded, "fairly oozing an incurable antipathy to games of chance and cunning?"

The bride drew herself up stiffly. "I am Mrs. John Birdey Doggett," she said, striving for a hauteur the name will not sustain.

"I forgot about her," whined Doggett. "After all, we haven't been married twenty or thirty years. We've only been married eleven hours."

CHAPTER TWENTY-TWO

What Cocktail Party?

I'M NOT SO STUPID as to believe that the cocktail party in 'The Cocktail Party' is actually a cocktail party," Grace Sheldon told me the other day at a cocktail party that was unquestionably a cocktail party. "What do *you* think it is?"

I was all wariness in a moment. Ever since the distinguished Mr. T. S. Eliot's widely discussed play came to town, I have been cornered at parties by women, and men, who seem intent on making me say what I think "The Cocktail Party" means, so they can cry "Great God, how naïve!" and then go around telling people that I probably don't even know the significance of the pumpkin in "Cinderella." I have learned to spar for time, with a counter-question of my own. "Do you believe in the innocence of the innocents in 'The Innocents'?" I asked Grace Sheldon.

Grace finished her Martini and looked around for the man in the white coat with the cocktail tray. "The only thing I am sure of," she said, "is the death of the salesman in 'Death of a Salesman.' I'm sure he dies and is supposed to be dead."

"You're just an old positivist," I said.

"The point is whether Eliot was impelled to write the play by forces beyond his control and cognizance," chimed in Charles Endless, joining us and waving his empty highball glass. "I presume you're talking about *the* play." Endless is forever repeating the critical judgments of his psychiatrist, Dr. Karl Wix, and embroidering them with the skeins of his own prejudices. "There is no such thing as the power of conscious selection in the creative writer," Charles went on. "I should say that the psychic inspiration of 'The Cocktail Party' was the consequence of something Eliot had done, whereas 'The Turn of the

Screw'—or 'The Innocents,' if you prefer to call it that—is clear proof of Henry James's conscious un-awareness of something he had *not* done."

"Something important, of course," I annotated.

"Vastly," underlined Endless. "Observe the size of the symbols these two writers have been impelled to select from the stockpile of literary devices and properties: the holy cross and the dark tower."

"I haven't seen 'The Sign of the Screw,' and I don't want to talk about it," said Grace. "I want to find out what Mr. Thurber thinks 'The Cocktail Party' is about. I'm not interested in what Dr. Wix thinks was the matter with Henry James."

"Great God!" cried Charles. "The woman seeks narrative sense in the sheerest mechanism of expiation!"

"I do not," said Grace, taking another Martini from the hovering cocktail tray.

Endless bowed with what he believed to be eighteenth-century grace, and was about to set off to find more congenial intellectual companionship when Malcolm Codd said something that arrested him. Codd, who had appeared quietly, as usual, from nowhere, wore glasses with flesh-colored rims and sipped furtively at a glass of milk. "Yes?" said Charles irritably, turning on him.

"I say," Codd said, "that anyone is indiscreet who tells what he thinks the play means. It is clearly one of those projection techniques, like the ink blots that are now all the vogue with psychiatrists. What the spots and the play mean to you is the thumbprint of your persona, the signature of your psyche, a history of your past, a key to your bedroom, a portrait of your ego in Technicolor. I would no more think of telling you what 'The Cocktail Party' meant to me last Saturday afternoon than I would think of telling you last night's dream."

"You should have read either a great deal more or a great deal less than you have," Charles said.

I decided to color the dialogue with some rhythms of my own, since they always annoy Charles. "What makes you think, Codd, that the meaning of the play to you, or last night's dream, is sure to show a sinister significance?" I asked.

Charles stared at me in horror. "Great God!" he cried. "Are you looking for the bluebird of happiness? Do you think there are actually hinges on chimneys so the stars can get by? Do you believe Love will slay the dragon and live happily ever after?"

I was as cool as steel. "I believe in the sudden deep greenness of summer," I said. In the fifteen years I have known Charles, his skepticism has always shattered against my affirmation, and he knows it.

"Bah!" he said, turning grandly on his heel, and bumping into old Mrs. Weaver, who is convinced that Eliot wrote the play in his sleep.

What Cocktail Party?

"Goddam it," she said, "look where you're going."

Mrs. Codd laughed. Since she never says anything, I hadn't noticed she was there.

"He is lost beyond saving," Codd said, taking his wife's arm and leading her away.

ONE ALWAYS KNOWS Grace Sheldon is there. She began to chew on it again. "I don't know you well enough to tell you what Dr. Wix thinks 'Gentlemen Prefer Blondes' is about," she said, watching Ruth Endless dive out of a cloud of women, strafe her husband briefly, and disappear behind a cliff of laughing men. "Or rather," she went on, "what Charles says Dr. Wix thinks it means. But you still haven't told me what *you* think of 'The Cocktail Party.' "

I laughed a laugh that was not actually a laugh.

"What *don't* you think it means, then?" she put in helpfully.

I circled around this for a moment. "Do you mean what Eliot is *intentionally* not saying, or what he just *happens* not to have said?" I asked, with enormous tidiness. She looked bewildered and I tried to clear it up for her, and for me. "Let me put it this way," I said. "No playwright has ever deliberately said 'Kings wear oysters in their shoes.' This line has not been left out, however, in the sense that it has been *rejected*. It is certainly not what Eliot is *not* saying. If we

223

charged him with it, he might quite properly reply, 'I would never not say that!' "

Grace Sheldon sighed, and robbed the passing tray of another drink. "Then what is it he isn't saying?" she wailed. "What is it he doesn't mean to mean?"

"My dear lady," I said, "if we were to discuss what he does not mean, we would find ourselves discussing what some other particular play does mean, since I am persuaded that what he is not saying has been said in some identifiable drama, and just as vehemently as he has not said it, if not so eloquently. The question is —what other play?"

Grace made a desperate stab at it. " 'Candida'?" she whispered.

I am afraid I sneered. Grace can be extraordinarily obtuse. "I am not privy to what Eliot is not saying," I said coldly, "but I will stake my sacred honor that he is not not saying what 'Candida' says."

Grace glanced at her watch. "I wish everybody were as simple as Shaw," she said. "I'm going home." And she went.

RUTH ENDLESS descended on me with Archie Kess in tow. "Archie has a theory about Peter Quilpe in 'The Cocktail Party,' " she said. "Archie thinks Quilpe is not really the wife's lover but the husband's fantasy of the kind of lover she would pick if she picked one."

"A degradation symbol?" I asked.

"Exactly," said Archie. "Eliot has given the word 'Quilpe' the same force as our 'twerp' or 'drip.' If he had meant the character to be real, he would have called him Querringhouse, or Quillingham, or Quartermaine."

I turned this over in my mind. Then Ruth said, "I happen to know that Quilpe is based on an actual person Eliot can't stand named Sweeney, or Prufrock, or some such name. Just as Julia in the show is Lady Serena Carnarvon, or somebody, who once hit Eliot with a paper dart at a musicale in London."

Archie kept nodding and grinning, and I snarled at him, "If it gives you two any satisfaction to find the paper snow of personal retaliation in this magnificent blizzard of poetic thought, I hope all the radiators in your part of Hell go thrump."

"All the time?" asked Archie.

I walked away from them and joined Betty Logan and Tom Frayne.

"For God's sake, Betty," Frayne was saying, gesturing with his cigarette, "say the Psychiatrist is Ambition, or Hope, or God, or Escapism, or Dedication, or the Father Image, or the Death Urge, or the Oedipus Complex, or a snatch of song you can't get out of your mind, but don't stand there and try to tell me he is an actual, carnate, human male psychiatrist. Can you imagine such a well-bred and cultured English psychiatrist—for that is what he would be if he were mortal—*crashing* a cocktail party in London?"

"What makes you think it is a cocktail party?" I asked coolly. "Eliot himself says—"

"I don't care what Eliot himself says," snapped Tom. "Eliot has missed a great many of the meanings in his play—wasn't that obvious to you when you saw it?"

"I wouldn't say 'obvious,'" I said. "I would say it nagged and nibbled at the rind of my consciousness."

"What do *you* think the play is about? What do *you* think it means?" asked Betty.

I decided to withdraw down a murky bypass. "The identity of the third murderer in 'Macbeth' has puzzled Shakespearean scholars for more than three centuries," I said. "Would it impair or increase your pleasure in the great tragedy if you found out who he actually is, or was?"

"It wouldn't make any difference to me," Betty said.

"What are you driving at, Thurber?" asked Tom.

"The Catonian Trium," I said. "'The Cocktail Party' is plainly a revaluation of the theory of Cato the Elder that two primary identities can sustain an unidentifiable third. That is, the *duum* differs from the *unum* in that it can absorb, without distortion of meaning, the introduction of an unknown, or mysterious, or debatable third."

What Cocktail Party?

"Naturally," said Tom with crisp impatience. "Everybody knows that. But it doesn't apply here. You are adding the Psychiatrist to Julia and Alex when, as a matter of fact, *they* are added to him. You don't seem to understand what identity is being concealed."

I found myself in the embarrassing position of being routed in an argument involving a theory I had made up. "He'll debauch you, Betty," I said, and retreated from the field.

WHEN THE ELIOT play begins to burn at the edges of a cocktail party, it spreads rapidly through the room, igniting every tongue, including the tongues of those ladies and gentlemen who haven't seen the play and don't intend to, or can hardly wait. On my way to the front hall, after waving goodbye to my hostess, I overheard a young man telling a pretty girl that the play is a hoax, the secret of whose anagrammatic scheme had been figured out by his roommate at Harvard, a brilliant chap named Buzz Walkley. As I passed into the hall, Judge Henneman trotted out of the lavatory, hardly able to breathe, as usual, and seized my arm. "What's fellow up to?" he wheezed. "Study of the female element in the human male," I explained. "Buncombe," he wheezed. "Discipline breaking down all over world." He stood there, gripping my arm and trying to breathe for a full minute. Then he let go and tottered back to the controversy.

227

I turned to find Edgeley, the butler, waiting with my hat and coat and stick. "What do *you* make of it, Edgeley?" I asked.

He helped me on with my coat. "It's another variant of the prickly-pear theme, I should say," he ventured, "if I'm not perhaps being a bit too basic."

"Not at all," I said. "I'm afraid some of us have been much too high in the superstructure to see the fundamentals clearly." We walked to the door.

"Your point is prettily taken," he said.

I thanked him.

"There is an ancient Latin saying," he went on, "which, freely translated, goes like this: 'If my ship burn at sea, then who shall know its destination save the stars and God?' "

"Who indeed?" I said cautiously. I thought I detected a faint whiff of kirsch on his breath.

"My colleague, Huntington," he continued, "has hit it off rather sharply, I think—but I am boring you."

"Not at all," I told him. "What does Huntington say?"

"Huntington says, 'It is desolater than you think.' " He opened the door for me. "Quite keen, don't you agree?"

"Very," I said.

What Cocktail Party?

I WENT OUT and Edgeley closed the door slowly and softly behind me. I stood a moment on the stoop, wondering vaguely about his background. A cab turned the corner and I waved it down. When I got in, I glanced at the driver's identification card and saw that his name was Louis Sandek. He turned around and looked at me thoughtfully. "You know something?" he said. I took fifty cents out of my pocket, gave it to him, got out of the cab, and slammed the door shut. He shrugged and drove off. It was twelve blocks to my hotel, but I walked. I was in no mood to listen to the Sandek version.

CHAPTER TWENTY-THREE

Joyeux Noël, Mr. Durning

I THINK I would have allowed the illicit merchandise to lapse into forfeiture if it had come from anyone except Maria and Olympy, but I couldn't let them down. I could have written them, of course, saying that I had received their *joli cadeau,* but it is awkward to thank someone for a bottle of liqueur if you don't know what kind of liqueur it is. Thus it was that I replied to Mr. Durning's form letter, received ten days before Christmas five years ago.

If you received one of these notifications, and I understand that hundreds, or perhaps thousands, were sent out, you were probably sensible enough to give up the struggle for your bottle by the middle of February, but I am made of a sterner curiosity. Once the game was afoot, I—but let us begin with Mr. Durning's first letter:

231

Thurber Country

TREASURY DEPARTMENT
BUREAU OF CUSTOMS
NEW YORK 4, N. Y.

IN REPLY REFER TO:
Seiz. #41802
Det. #3173-M-48
DECEMBER 14, 1948

Mr. and Mrs. James Thurber,
The New Yorker,
25 West 43rd Street,
N. Y. City 18, N. Y.

SIR AND MADAM:

There has been placed under seizure the merchandise set forth below which arrived in the mails from Mr./Mrs. Sementzoff, France; contained in a package addressed to you.

(1) bottle—1/5 gal. size—Alc. Liqueur.

You are informed that any postal union (regular) mail articles or parcel post package received from abroad which is found to contain spirituous, vinous, malted, fermented, or other intoxicating liquor of any kind, is prohibited importation in the mails and is subject to seizure and forfeiture under the provisions of section 340, title 18, U.S. Code, and section 593 (b) of Tariff Act of 1930.

If you desire to obtain possession of this liquor you must furnish to the Law Division of this office, ROOM

Joyeux Noël, Mr. Durning

318 CUSTOMHOUSE, BOWLING GREEN, NEW YORK, NEW YORK, a statement setting forth the facts surrounding the importation indicating whether the same is for your personal use or for commercial purposes, that the merchandise, if released, will not be replaced in the mails, and that notification has been given to the shipper that the importation of intoxicating liquors through the mails is prohibited. Upon receipt of such statement you will be advised of the terms upon which the liquor will be released to you.

Unless the liquor in question is taken possession of by you within a reasonable time, the same will be disposed of according to law.

Respectfully,

HARRY M. DURNING,
Collector of Customs
By: J. P. SHARAGHER
Actg. Dep. Coll.

NOW, THIS DOCUMENT smelled to heaven of potential prolixity and proliferation, and my family and friends, knowing my tendency toward querulous impatience in protracted official give-and-take, warned me to ignore it. But I thought of Olympy and Maria. The last time my wife and I saw them was in the troubled spring of 1938, when we waved good-bye to them as we drove away from the Villa Tamisier, in Juan-les-Pins. I later wrote a small memorial to

Thurber Country

Maria's cooking and character, and to the wild aban-
don and quiet fortitude of her husband the day he
drove my Ford sedan—and me—into a telephone pole.
We heard from them during the first year of the Occu-
pation, in a letter addressed to me in care of the New
York *Herald*, New York, U.S.A. They were in good
health but sad spirits, and somehow deeply concerned
about our safety (in that most dangerous of war fronts
—Connecticut). We sent them boxes of food from
time to time, and our repeated assurances that we
were well and safe, but Maria was apparently not
convinced. The day the American troops arrived, she
wrote us, she ran out into the streets of Juan-les-Pins
and demanded *nouvelles de M. et Mme. Thurber*
from a passing column of soldiers. A captain—who
didn't know the Thurbers from Adam and Eve—
shouted back at her that we were carrying ourselves
well, and Maria was at last relieved of her grand anxiety. I have often wished that I could thank that gallant officer for his quick and thoughtful good tidings
about Maria's *Monsieur et Madame à New York*.

Yes, thinking about Maria and Olympy, I had to
get that bottle. My first brave letter, together with its
tangled consequences, follows, for your information
and guidance:

Joyeux Noël, Mr. Durning

WEST CORNWALL, CONN.
DECEMBER 17, 1948

The Law Division,
Office of the Collector,
Room 318, Customhouse,
Bowling Green,
New York, N. Y.

GENTLEMEN:

I am writing in connection with a letter of December 14th from Mr. Harry M. Durning, Collector of Customs, sent to Mr. and Mrs. James Thurber, c/o *The New Yorker* Magazine, 25 West 43rd Street, New York City. Mr. Durning's letter asks me to refer to "Seiz. #41802 and Det. #3173-M-48."

The bottle of alcoholic liqueur is intended as a Christmas gift to Mrs. Thurber and myself, and was shipped from France by Mr. and Mrs. Olympy Sementzoff, who worked as our gardener and cook in France some ten years ago. They are obviously not familiar with U.S. customs restrictions on shipments of alcoholic beverages from abroad.

I am advising the shippers of the customs regulations that obtain in this case, and asking them to abide by these regulations in the future.

The bottle is intended for the private use of Mrs. Thurber and myself and will be used for no commercial purpose. If and when it is released to us, it will not be replaced in the mails.

I await your further instructions in this matter, and regret the inconvenience it has caused you.

Respectfully yours,
JAMES THURBER

TREASURY DEPARTMENT
BUREAU OF CUSTOMS
NEW YORK 4, N. Y.

IN REPLY REFER TO:
GM/22
Seizure #41802
DECEMBER 30, 1948

Mr. James Thurber,
West Cornwall, Conn.
SIR:

Addressee: Mr. & Mrs. James Thurber
Merchandise: 1 bottle 1/5 gal. Alc. Liqueur
Sum to be deposited: $3.56 (total)

Receipt is acknowledged of your letter of December 17, 1948 regarding the merchandise listed above which arrived in the mail and which has been placed under seizure for violation of the customs revenue laws.

To secure the release of this merchandise from Customs we require that there be deposited with us the sum above stated. This payment may be made by cer-

Joyeux Noël, Mr. Durning

tified check or postal money order payable to the Collector of Customs. You are also advised that in addition to our terms of release which include the payment of the above listed sum, before the merchandise finally may be released, it will be necessary for you to present to this office a state permit therefor from the Connecticut State Liquor Authority at Hartford. Upon receipt of the permit and the payment above listed, the liqueur will be forwarded to you by express, charges collect.

We request that you act promptly in this matter to secure the release of this merchandise: otherwise, it will be disposed of as provided by law.

Respectfully,
HARRY M. DURNING, COLLECTOR
By: ALFRED H. GOLDEN
Assistant Solicitor

WEST CORNWALL, CONN.
JANUARY 5, 1949

Mr. Harry M. Durning,
Collector of Customs,
Bureau of Customs,
New York 4, N. Y.

DEAR MR. DURNING:

In reference to GM/22 and Seizure #41802, and your letter of December 30, '1948, in reply to my own letter of December 17, I am this day writing for a permit from the Connecticut State Liquor Authority, which I will forward promptly when received, together with a postal money order for $3.56.

Sincerely yours,
JAMES THURBER

WEST CORNWALL, CONN.
JANUARY 5, 1949

Connecticut Liquor Authority,
Hartford, Connecticut

GENTLEMEN:

I have been advised in a letter just received from Mr. Harry M. Durning, Collector of Customs in New York, that I must submit to him a Connecticut permit in order to obtain the release of a 1/5 gallon of alcoholic spirits now under seizure in New York. All other requirements set forth by Mr. Durning have been satisfied by me. The bottle under seizure will be forwarded to me by express on submission of the proper permit from your authority.

Thanking you for your prompt consideration in this matter, and with best season's wishes, I am

Sincerely yours,
JAMES THURBER

Joyeux Noël, Mr. Durning

LIQUOR CONTROL COMMISSION
STATE OF CONNECTICUT
HARTFORD

JANUARY 10, 1949

James Thurber
West Cornwall, Connecticut

DEAR SIR:

Receipt is acknowledged of your communication of January 5, 1949 with reference to alcoholic liquor for your personal consumption which you desire to import into the State.

With reference to this situation, you are advised that it is necessary to apply for and receive a permit for the importation of this type of merchandise. We are enclosing, herewith, blank forms of application, no one of which may be for more than five gallons.

Before executing these applications, the State Tax Commissioner, Excise Division, State Office Building, Hartford, Connecticut should be advised as to the type of beverage to be imported; if any wine is included, the alcoholic percentage and whether "sparkling" or "still"; and they will immediately advise you as to the amount of tax due. The applications should then be executed and forwarded to the Tax Department with a check in the amount of the taxes and, when received, that department will then forward them to us with the certification that the taxes have been paid and we will, in turn, issue an Import Certificate to you which must be forwarded by you to whatever transportation company is to transport the merchandise into Connecticut. This Import Certificate must accompany the merchandise in transit and must be delivered to the importer at the time of the delivery of the merchandise. Upon receipt of the alcoholic beverages, the Import Certificate must of necessity be returned to this department.

If there is any further information which you desire on the subject, we shall be very glad to advise you upon request.

Very truly yours,

RICHARD H. PINNEY
Executive Assistant
Liquor Control Commission

P.S. The state tax on whiskey is computed as $1.00 per wine gallon.

WEST CORNWALL, CONN.
FEBRUARY 4, 1949

The State Tax Commissioner,
Excise Division,
State Office Building,
Hartford, Connecticut
DEAR SIR:

On December 30, 1948, I was advised by the New York Customs authorities that they are holding one

Joyeux Noël, Mr. Durning

bottle 1/5 gallon alcoholic liqueur, shipped to me, in
ignorance of our laws, by M. and Mme. Olympy
Sementzoff from France. I was instructed to notify
the Connecticut Liquor Authority, which informed
me, in enclosing applications for release, that I should
describe, as hereinabove, the nature and contents of
the bottle in question. I have set down all that I know
about it. The New York Customs demands $3.56 as
their fee for release. I await your advice as to the
proper tax due in this state, in full and helpless confidence that the aforementioned Christmas present will
be disposed of as contraband before a man of my age
can possibly satisfy all the documentary requirements.
Nevertheless, I am going to try to get it.

M. Sementzoff is a White Russian, and I trust that
the purity of his loyalty to France need not be established by the F.B.I. or any other organization.

Respectfully yours,
JAMES THURBER

STATE OF CONNECTICUT

TAX DEPARTMENT

470 CAPITOL AVENUE

HARTFORD 15, CONNECTICUT

IN REPLY REFER TO:

Beverage Tax Section

FEBRUARY 8, 1949

Mr. James Thurber,

West Cornwall,

Connecticut.

DEAR SIR:

Receipt is acknowledged of your letter of the 4th received in this office this morning.

We wish to advise that Connecticut state tax on 1/5 gallon of liqueur is $0.20.

If you will forward your remittance in the amount of $0.20 to cover the tax due on the liqueur that is being held by the New York Customs for you, together with the completed applications sent you by the Liquor Control Commission, we will certify payment of the tax to the Liquor Commission who will then forward you a release.

Respectfully yours,

WILLIAM F. CONNELLY

Tax Commissioner

By: ERNEST S. GOODRICH

Director, Excise Division

Joyeux Noël, Mr. Durning

THE BRITISH COLONIAL HOTEL,
NASSAU, BAHAMAS,
19 FEBRUARY 1949

Mr. William F. Connelly
Tax Commissioner
Hartford, Conn.
Attn: Mr. Ernest S. Goodrich,
  Director, Excise Division

Re: Beverage Tax Section

DEAR MR. CONNELLY:

In connection with your letter of February 8th sent by Mr. Goodrich, I am enclosing a check for twenty cents ($.20), together with the necessary applications, in accordance with your instructions as to the procedure for gaining the release of the bottle of liqueur now being held by the New York Customs authorities.

I am enclosing an American air-mail stamp in order that the release from the Connecticut State Liquor Control Commission may be expedited and I am taking the liberty of requesting your kindness in sending this stamp along to them, so that the release may be sent air mail to me, c/o The British Colonial, Nassau, the Bahamas. A letter sent by ordinary mail might take weeks in getting here and I am unfamiliar with the period of time regarded as reasonable by the New York Customs officials.

Thanking you for your help in this matter,

Sincerely yours,

JAMES THURBER

243

LIQUOR CONTROL COMMISSION
STATE OF CONNECTICUT
HARTFORD

FEBRUARY 24, 1949

James G. Thurber,
R.F.D.,
West Cornwall, Conn.

DEAR SIR:

Enclosed herewith is Import Certificate #1627 authorizing the importation into the State of Connecticut, for your personal consumption, of LIQUEUR.

The Import Certificate must accompany the merchandise in transit *and be delivered to you with the merchandise.*

Upon receipt of the merchandise, the Import Certificate *enclosed must be returned by you to this department.*

Very truly yours,

RICHARD H. PINNEY
Executive Assistant
Liquor Control Commission

The above certificate mailed to British Colonial Hotel, Nassau, Bahamas, as requested. (Air Mail)

Joyeux Noël, Mr. Durning

THE BRITISH COLONIAL HOTEL,
NASSAU, BAHAMAS,
3 MARCH 1949

Mr. Harry M. Durning,
Collector of Customs,
Bureau of Customs,
New York 4, N. Y.
DEAR MR. DURNING:

With reference to GM/22 and Seizure #41802, and to your letters of December 14 and December 30, 1948, I am, pursuant to your direction, enclosing my check for $3.56, together with the Import Certificate just issued to me by the Liquor Control Commission of the State of Connecticut.

The Commission has advised me that the Import Certificate must accompany the shipment of the merchandise so that I may return the Certificate to the Commission when I receive it. It is my desire to conform, in full, with all the requirements of your office and those of the Connecticut authorities concerned.

There has been some unavoidable delay in gathering together all the necessary releases and certificates, but I trust I have not exceeded the time limit placed upon the holding of the merchandise. In the past two and a half months I have developed a profound curiosity as to the actual contents of the merchandise.

I understand from a recent newspaper article that

your office has been overburdened by the receipt of illegal shipments of alcoholic spirits from friends of Americans in France and other countries who are unaware that their expressions of good feeling are contrary to statutes of the United States. I regret that I have innocently added to your work and to your problems, and I assure you that I have made every effort to prevent the recurrence of this situation.

Sincerely yours,

JAMES THURBER

P.S. I understand that the merchandise is to be shipped to me at West Cornwall, Conn., but it has occurred to me that it may be receivable only by myself or by Mrs. Thurber personally. If this is the case, I will not be in West Cornwall until March 8th. There is, however, always someone at my home to receive the shipment.

WEST CORNWALL, CONN.
APRIL 5, 1949

Mr. Harry M. Durning,
Collector of Customs,
Bureau of Customs,
New York 4, N. Y.
DEAR MR. DURNING:

In further reference to GM/22 and Seizure #41802.

I wrote you on March 3rd, air mail from Nassau,

the Bahamas, enclosing my personal check for $3.56, in final satisfaction of the stipulations of your own office and of the various Connecticut State authorities involved by law in the transaction regarding the shipment to Mrs. Thurber and myself of a Christmas gift from M. and Mme. Olympy Sementzoff in France. I am not yet in receipt of the 1/5 gallon of alcoholic liqueur that is being held under seizure by your office, unless the act of forfeiture has already been consummated.

In the fear that the shipment may have been delayed because of some fault or failure of my own, I have gone back over the voluminous correspondence in this matter, searching for possible error on my part, and I have discovered that you asked for a certified check or postal money order and that I had said I would send the tax in the form of the money order. Circumstances operated to place difficulties in my way, since I was in Nassau, where American money orders are unavailable and the certification of checks was not easy to arrange.

If the merchandise has not yet been forfeited I shall be glad to substitute a certified check in the amount of $3.56 for the check I sent you on March 3rd.

When and if the bottle is received by me, I want to write the shippers to thank them again for the gift, and I should like to be able to state the precise brand or type of liqueur. Otherwise they might suspect that

Thurber Country

I had never actually received the present, and this would add further distress to their present embarrassment, which results from their knowledge that their Christmas gift was shipped in contravention, however innocent, of our statutes and regulations.

The Connecticut State Liquor Control Commission has instructed me to return the Import Certificate when I receive the shipment. If the merchandise has, in fact, been forfeited I do not know how to comply with this particular instruction.

My curiosity as to the actual contents of the bottle has not abated, and I would greatly appreciate it if, no matter how this transaction eventuates, you would identify the liqueur for me.

I fully appreciate the problems you have to deal with in the case of the thousands of such shipments mentioned in the newspaper article I read on the subject. This one bottle has very nearly driven me crazy.

Respectfully yours,

JAMES THURBER

Joyeux Noël, Mr. Durning

WEST CORNWALL, CONN.
APRIL 6, 1949

Mr. Harry M. Durning,
Collector of Customs,
Bureau of Customs,
New York 4, N. Y.

DEAR MR. DURNING:

GM/22 and Seizure #41802.

In reference to my letter of yesterday, April 5, I regret to say that it was written and mailed during the absence of Mrs. Thurber, who, upon her return, explained that you had accepted and put through my check of March 3rd in the amount of $3.56, and that the cancelled check had arrived in my bank statement on April 2nd. She further pointed out that the delay in shipment of the bottle of liqueur is no doubt due to the railway-express strike, which still obtains at this writing.

Please ignore my letter of yesterday and accept my apologies for adding to the confusion and to the considerable dossier in this matter which I have been at fault in amplifying.

Respectfully yours,
JAMES THURBER

P.S. If the Christmas gift does not arrive before Easter, I will be in Bermuda, but the shipment will be received by my caretaker, Mr. Ben Tuller, who

249

Thurber Country

has instructions to forward the Import Certificate to the Connecticut Liquor Authority on my behalf.

TREASURY DEPARTMENT
BUREAU OF CUSTOMS
NEW YORK 4, N. Y.

IN REPLY REFER TO:
GJM:z/22
Seizure No. 41802
APRIL 12, 1949

Mr. James Thurber
West Cornwall
Connecticut
SIR:

Reference is made to previous correspondence with this office relative to a shipment of alcoholic beverage consigned to you through the international mails in violation of the United States Code, title 18, sections 1716 and 545, covered by the above seizure number.

This office is in receipt of your remittance in accordance with the terms imposed for the release of this merchandise to you. However, the present express embargo will undoubtedly result in a delay in the receipt of the shipment by you.

Respectfully,
HARRY M. DURNING, COLLECTOR
By: ALFRED H. GOLDEN
Assistant Solicitor

Joyeux Noël, Mr. Durning

On April 22nd, six days after I had sailed for Bermuda, and one hundred and twenty-nine days after the original form letter from Mr. Durning, the merchandise arrived at West Cornwall, Connecticut, intact, according to Ben Tuller, who wrote me air mail that same day, enclosing the Import Certificate, which, it turned out, had to be signed by me. There were express charges of ninety-five cents on the merchandise, which Tuller paid. He was afraid that I might not return the Import Certificate to Hartford within the period of five days after the acceptance of the shipment, as prescribed by statute. I think I managed it, in spite of the unfortunate fact that his letter was first delivered, by mistake, to Waterlot, in Southampton Parish, instead of to Waterville, in Paget East, where I was staying. The Import Certificate, because of the gravity of its warning and the nobility of its language, deserves to be read into this record, and it follows in full, or almost in full:

This certifies that James G. Thurber of R.F.D., West Cornwall, Conn., having paid the tax prescribed by SUB-SECTION (b) of SECTION 986e, 1939 SUPPLEMENT TO THE GENERAL STATUTES, AS AMENDED, is authorized to import into the STATE OF CONNECTICUT ⅙ Gal. LIQUEUR from Mr. and Mrs. Olympy Sementzoff, Juan-les-Pins, France, for his own use and consumption and not for resale. This certificate must be returned to Liquor Control Commission by person to whom issued within five (5) days after receipt of contents represented.

I WILL spare you my two letters, in French, to Maria and Olympy, the first thanking them for a gift I had not yet received and cautioning them not to do it again, the second announcing that the *joli cadeau de Noël* had arrived at my home five days after *Pâques*. I explained that I would be *en séjour à Bermuda* until late in June, but that I would drink to their health and happiness on the Fourth of July.

Maria and Olympy will understand. After all, the French are by no means inexperienced in the long and labyrinthine processes of officialdom, complete with symbols, seals, signatures, and the satisfaction of statutes and stipulations.

Oh, yes, I almost forgot. It was a bottle of Cointreau.

(Consignee's Note: Shortly after the preceding correspondence appeared in *The New Yorker,* I received a nice letter from Mr. Durning, enclosing an official check for two dollars. It seems that, somewhere along the line, I was inadvertently overcharged that amount.)

See No Weevil

I PROBABLY WOULD NEVER have known about the "Thurberia Weevil" or the Thurberia plant, either, if Clarence R. Peterson of Brooklyn hadn't sent me a report on them taken from the pages of the *Federal Register,* a publication of the U.S. Department of Agriculture that deals with American plants and the pests that threaten them. If any insect is trailing the arbutus, or creeping up on the Virginia

creeper, agents of the Department photograph and
fingerprint it, give it a serial number, and keep it under surveillance. Otherwise vegetation would disappear from the Republic and some enormous caterpil-
lar would take over where Senator McCarthy left off.

The report from the *Federal Register* that Mr.
Peterson sent me contains the glad tidings, for cotton
growers and Thurberia weevils, that the 1926 quarantine on the *Anthonomus grandis thurberiae Pierce*
has been lifted. It seems that my cousin, the weevil,
has turned out to be a harmless insect, no more dangerous to the American cotton crop than the luna moth
is to the Brazilian Air Force. I don't know who Pierce
is, by the way, or how he happened to pop up in the
name of the Thurber weevil, but it may be that he was
the agent who kept Thurberia under surveillance for
twenty-five years. If I had spent the best years of my
life tailing a weevil, I would certainly expect some
permanent recognition. I don't know who Thurber is,
either. My own branch of the family has never been
very good at entomology or botany. This Thurber may
have been an entomologist who discovered the Thurberia plant, or wild cotton, while hunting for weevils,
or he may have been a botanist who discovered the
weevil while hunting for the wild cotton plant. It is
a kind of ordinary weed found in hot, arid areas of
the Southwest, and it is not actually cotton, and it isn't
terribly wild. The Thurberia weevil likes to inhabit

See No Weevil

the Thurberia plant, anyway, but twenty-five years of research have shown that the weevil is not really a pest at all. His famous cousin, the boll weevil, is a great destroyer of cotton, but Thurberia wouldn't cross the road to examine a cotton plant, let alone try to destroy it. I don't know why it took a quarter of a century to find this out, but the wheels of government move slowly.

THURBERIA, to be sure, is not the only plant named after a man. Literally hundreds of flowers and weeds have been named for their discoverers: forsythia for Forsythe, zinnia for Zinn, dahlia for Dahl, fuchsia for Fuchs, and so on. There are even muehlenbeckia and puschkinia, I found in glancing through *The New Garden Encyclopedia*. This dictionary of flora, first published in 1936, contains 1380 pages, but Thurberia, the wild cotton, isn't mentioned in it.

I DON'T KNOW what Mrs. Thurber thought or said when Thurber came home one evening and told her that he had discovered a kind of scrubby desert plant and was going to have it named after him, but if he had belonged to my branch of the family (Thurberia Columbus) the conversation would have gone something like this...

"If I had it to do over again," said Mrs. Thurber, "I wouldn't have married a desert botanist. I don't

255

know why you have to go in for things like mesquite and toadbush, when everybody else's husband is finding such lovely flowers—"

"Forsythe and Wister, if you mean them, are deciduous men," Thurber cut in, "and I happen to be xerophilous. You could have done worse—you might have married Hubbard and had that squash named after you."

"Yes, but if I had married Wilson, the ornithologist, I could have had a thrush named after me."

"Supposing you had married Newton," her husband said, "then you would have had a fig cookie named after you. And how about Mrs. Comstock?"

"I don't know any Mrs. Comstock," said Mrs. Thurber.

"Comstock discovered the Comstock mealy bug," the botanist said. "It infests the catalpas and is also found on the magnolias, and it—"

"I don't care if it dances on hydrangeas," snapped Mrs. Thurber. "I don't want to hear about it. I don't see why you couldn't have gone out and found a new kind of lilac or lily-of-the-valley."

The tired botanist lit a cigarette. "Why don't *you* go out and discover a rose?" he asked her. "After all, Dorothy Perkins did."

This kind of thing, in certain branches of the Thurber family, could go on for weeks, as it must have in the Muehlenbeck family, when Mrs. Muehlenbeck

See No Weevil

found out that muehlenbeckia is only a kind of buck-wheat.

I do not like to dwell on what happened when Thurber came home one evening, with the worried look that Mrs. Thurber knew so well.

"What's the matter?" asked Mrs. Thurber apprehensively. "Have you discovered a new kind of non-flowering buzzard bush?"

He dropped into a chair. "No," he said. "Do you remember that weevil I found on the Thurberia plant?"

She sighed. "Yes," she said, "but I keep trying to forget it." Her eyes brightened. "Has it been taken suddenly extinct?" she asked hopefully.

"No, it isn't that," he said wearily. "Something else has happened to it."

"Are you going to sit there and tell me that Pierce has taken full credit for it?" she demanded. "I always knew he would, and I told you—"

"Pierce hasn't taken credit for anything," he said irritably. "Thurberia has turned out to be innocuous. It's not even mischievous. Its quarantine has been lifted, if you have to know."

His wife sat forward in her chair. "I knew that would happen," she said. "Don't you realize that hundreds of scientists have seen that weevil during the past hundred years, and that you were the only one foolish enough to stop and classify it? Now you've

257

got yourself stuck with a weevil that isn't even dangerous, a weevil that lives on wild cotton, the most ordinary bush in the desert. Jane Forsythe was telling me just the other day that it's as common as false fleabane. When you were out hunting for ticks and cactus and fungus, Jane's husband was discovering a beautiful golden flower—where are you going?"

Thurber had put on his hat and coat and walked to the door. With his hand on the knob, he turned and looked at his wife. "I'm going out to discover the Thurber mealy bug," he said coldly, "and when I do, I'm going to put it on the forsythia or on Jane Forsythe, I haven't decided which yet." And he went out and banged the door after him.

Mrs. Thurber lit a cigarette and sat for a while lost in thought. It suddenly dawned on her what Belle Pierce would do when she found out that the quarantine had been lifted on the "Thurberia Weevil." She would make her husband drop his name from it, leaving the Thurbers stuck with *Anthonomus grandis thurberiae.* Their name would stand there forever, in lower case, and become the laughing stock (*casus risus*) of the entomological world.

CHAPTER TWENTY-FIVE

The Pleasure Cruise, and How to Survive It

I T HAS OCCURRED to me that there may be persons here and there, young and inexperienced in the ways of the world, who might profit from my own personal TRAVEL HINTS, compiled after looking back on thirty-odd years of knocking about, or being knocked about, the globe. I don't mean the whole globe, of course. I have never been south of Trinidad, north of Quebec, east of Italy, or west of San Francisco, but within these rather roomy limits, I have been knocked about quite a bit.

My first hint—to the gentleman traveler—is a simple one. Never go anywhere without your wife. If your wife won't go, because the concert or canning season is on, or something of the sort, take your sister or your mother or your cousin. The American woman is indispensable in getting the tickets and reservations, packing and unpacking, mixing Bromo-Seltzers, fending off beautiful ladies who are traveling alone, and making herself useful generally. Hers is also the only sex that can successfully close a wardrobe trunk. If a man closes a wardrobe trunk, there is always a sharp snapping sound, caused by the breaking of something that will not bend, such as the handle of a mirror, or the stem of a Dunhill pipe, or the stopper of a perfume bottle. If a woman is deprived of her Chanel No. 5 during, say, a nineteen-day cruise, she will become irritable, and there is nothing more exasperating on a cruise, or anywhere else, than an irritable female companion.

Now that I have mentioned cruises, let us consider more closely the technique of the sea voyage. After the wife has closed the wardrobe trunk and called a taxi, it is only eight in the morning, and the ship doesn't sail till eleven. The husband will complain that it doesn't take three hours to get to a pier only eight blocks from their hotel. He will point out that they can get to Pier 58 in half an hour, with time to spare. He is right, it turns out, but it also turns out that he doesn't know where Pier 58 is. His wife has unfortunately left this one small detail up to him. He tells the taxi driver to take them to the foot of West 58th

The Pleasure Cruise, and How to Survive It

Street, but when they get there, it transpires that this is not the point of departure of their ship, the *Santa Maria*. It is the point of departure of the *J. B. Cathcart*, a coastwise fruit steamer bound for French Guiana. The taxi driver suggests that the *Santa Maria* probably sails from Brooklyn or Hoboken. The husband figures there is time to try both places, but his wife's sounder judgment prevails. She asks somebody —always an excellent idea—where Pier 58 is, and is told Pier 58 is at the foot of West 16th Street. It is, too.

On the way to the right destination, with time to spare—just as the husband had promised—the taxi driver suddenly has a hunch that the *Santa Maria* sails at 11 P.M., on Tuesdays, and not at 11 A.M., on Thursdays. This throws his male passenger into a panic. The seasoned woman traveler pays no attention to all this unnecessary masculine excitement. She leans back in the cab, closes her eyes and wonders if she forgot to pack her white piqué evening dress. Once aboard the ship, the wife (Ellen) tells her husband (George) that she has to unpack her light things right away or they will crush, and she asks him, for heaven's sake, to get deck chairs on the sunny and windless side of the ship immediately, before they are all gone, and also to make table reservations instantly, so they can have a table for two once in their lives, and not have to sit with a lot of strangers. George wanders away on these important errands and (1) runs into

The Pleasure Cruise, and How to Survive It

zigzagging from New York to St. Nazaire in heavy weather, and there was honorable excuse for my condition. I say I am "unlucky" enough to have a stomach of platinum, because the seasick turn to the unseasick on a ship for succor, sanctuary and salvation that are impossible to give. Once, on the Bermuda run—seventeen of us up and around on the second day, out of a passenger list of three hundred—I came upon a lone woman sprawled on a sofa in the library up forward, where rolling and pitching had flung her prostrate and forlorn. She lay on her hat and her right side; one shoe was off; her handbag was open on the floor, its contents scattered; her lipstick was smudged in such a way that she seemed to have bitten her own left cheek. I was appalled—sympathetic, gallant even, but appalled—and when I am appalled, my nervous system becomes an apparatus that, as the French say, *ne fonctionne pas.*

"Do something," she said in a faint, awful voice.

"Madam," I squeaked helplessly. I was unable to say anything, but I did something. I put her things back in her handbag and placed it on a table.

"I put your handbag on the table," I finally managed to croak.

"Do something," she said again, in the same voice. For a moment I considered putting her shoe back on, but like any other Ohio State man, I was restrained by the feeling that the act would be both insensitive and foolish. Then, I suddenly decided to put the shoe on the table with the handbag.

"Do something," she said, in a weaker tone. I staggered out of the library, hunted up a deck steward and told him about the lady and her extremity.

"Do something," I begged him. He just shook his head sadly. I rolled on my way, and came to the elevator that ran from A Deck down to E Deck and back. There was a woman there, frantically pressing the bell button. She was standing, and she had both shoes on, but she looked just as ghastly as the lost lady in the library. She grabbed my arm as I tried to walk by.

"E Deck. Quick!" she gasped.

"The elevator will be up——" I began and caught myself, but not in time. Her face took on a saffron hue.

"I'm sorry," I mumbled. She looked at me with the eyes of a stepped-on spaniel.

"E Deck," she said again. "Please."

I had to do something. I brushed past her and began pushing the bell button wildly. Then I turned and ran. I have often wondered, in my own low and agonized moments, if she made it.

Just what hint to give to the unseasick passenger who may be faced, during an ocean voyage, with crises and suffering similar to my own that terrible day, I frankly do not know. There are certain tortures that we unseasick passengers simply have to endure, I guess. I would appreciate it, though, if you don't go around saying that, in the emergencies I have described, I just "got the hell out." I did what I could. There will, of course, always be two schools of thought about that shoe, the school that contends I should have put it back on, and the school that insists I should have let it lie where I found it. Apparently nobody in the world but me would have put it on the table with the handbag. I can only say that if I had it all to do over again, I would still put the shoe on the table with the handbag.

If you travel much on ships you are bound, sooner or later, to run into Mrs. Abigail Pritchard, as I shall call her. She is not just one woman, but many; I have encountered at least fifteen of her. Mrs. Pritchard may be forty-five, or she may be seventy, but her average age, I should say, is about fifty-seven. She comes from Boston, Hartford, Germantown, Syracuse, Toledo, Chicago, Louisville, St. Louis, Denver, Sacramento, and both Portlands. She is a widow, fairly well off, whose children are happily married and the fathers, or mothers, of the prettiest and brightest youngsters in the world, and she has snapshots and anecdotes to prove it. She takes two Daiquiris before dinner and a highball afterwards, and smokes Players, on the ground that they are made of actual tobacco, whereas American cigarettes, in her opinion, are composed of rum, molasses, shredded cork, and factory sweepings. She prefers domestic Burgundies, however, because the so-called French vintages you find on ships are really only cheap Algerian wine that has been poured into genuine bottles labeled Pommard or Chablis. Mrs. Pritchard is full of interesting little anecdotes about the late Sir Harry Oakes, the late Richard Halliburton ("that dear boy"), a Colonel Grosvenor in Penang, the gifted Courtney girls (whoever they are), John Barrymore ("poor old Jack"), Heifetz, Houdini, Nell Brinkley, Anna Eva Fay, Percy Marmont, Maurice Costello ("the king of them all"), Kip Rhinelander, Mrs. O. H. P. Belmont, Struthers Burt, Ky Laffoon and anybody else whose name you happen to mention. Mrs. Pritchard is certain she saw Judge Crater in the Casino at Cannes in 1937, where he was known as Maltby or Goadby, or some such name. "How do you do, Judge Crater?" she said to him firmly. He started—there could be no doubt of that. "My name is Maltby (or Goadby), madam," the man said, and hurried away.

Mrs. Pritchard can invariably spot, aboard ship, professional gamblers, unmarried couples sharing the same stateroom, fugitives from justice, fingermen formerly in the employ of Al Capone, cocaine sniffers, bay-rum drinkers, professional men of dubious integrity, women who are mortally ill but don't know it, unhappy wives and gentlemen with phony foreign accents. It makes you nervous to talk to, or rather listen to, Mrs. Pritchard. You twist restlessly in your chair,

The Pleasure Cruise, and How to Survive It

confident that she has figured you for an absconder, a black-marketeer, or a white-slave trader. Mrs. Pritchard spends at least two months of every year on ships, but I often wonder why, since she suspects that there is skulduggery afoot from the chartroom to the hold. If the ship is even half an hour late in shoving off, she whispers that "Uncle Joe is behind this delay." She never clears this up, though, but merely shakes her head wisely, if you ask her what she means. She is sure the ship is going to put to sea with broken pumps, insufficient lifeboats, and a typhoid carrier among the crew. Two days out, she tells you she doesn't like the look of the saxophone player's complexion—he has something contagious, mark her words. The third day out she declares that the chief steward is secreting fifteen thousand pounds of roast beef, which he intends to sell to a syndicate in Port-au-Prince. It costs ten thousand dollars a day to operate a ship, she read in the *Reader's Digest*, and this ridiculous amount is due to thefts of supplies by the stewards.

Even the captain of the ship is not above her suspicion. She is positive that he forgot to order all those automobiles in the hold lashed down, and she knows they will roll to one side if a storm comes up, causing the ship to list, like the *Vestris*, and sink. Mrs. Pritchard loves to tell about the time the master of an ocean liner was seized with a heart attack while steering the boat—she still thinks he was an epileptic—and almost ran into an iceberg. But her favorite story is about the time she was on a West Indies cruise, and caught a glimpse of the captain one day. She recognized him instantly as a Major Quantrell (or Chantress, or some such name) wanted in Rangoon for the shooting of a missionary's daughter in a fashionable gambling house. Mrs. Pritchard points out that a captain's cabin is the perfect hide-out for fugitives from justice, since nobody is allowed in the cabin except the officers, and they are probably no better than they ought to be, themselves.

The young traveler will naturally expect old, experienced me to advise him how to avoid, or to deal with, Mrs. Pritchard. Well, you can't avoid her. Just dismiss that from your mind. She pops up from everywhere and out from behind everything. Even if you hid in the engine room, she would search you out. As for dealing with the old girl, I have invented a rather nasty game called Back Her in the Corner, which works wonders.

"You know the Hotel l'Aiglon in Roquebrune, of course?" I say to her, casually.

"To be sure," she replies. "That perfectly gorgeous view of the Bay of Monte Carlo at night!"

We both look dreamy.

"Ah, yes," I sigh, "and those wonderful sardines grilled in triple-sec!"

The Pleasure Cruise, and How to Survive It

"Yes, yes," she sighs, "those delicious sardines."

You see, she has to keep up a show of having been every place I have been. And here's where my game gets nasty.

"There isn't any Hotel l'Aiglon in Roquebrune," I say coldly, "and there aren't any sardines grilled in triple-sec."

She is furious. I have tricked her, and hell hath no fury like a woman tricked. She gives me a wide berth after that, not even nodding or smiling when I pass her on deck. I can get away with this little game because I am fifty-six,* but such conduct on the part of the *young* traveler would seem imprudent, disrespectful and ill-bred. You'll have to devise your own method of dealing with Mrs. Pritchard. You mustn't expect me to solve *all* your travel problems. And please don't write and ask me what to do in the event that you run into the gifted Courtney sisters. I simply do not know.

A few days out of New York (if you sailed from New York), printed copies of the passenger list are usually distributed, containing such names as Jowes, Qmith, Johnsob, Crazier, Aprker, Sommonx and Spider. It takes years of practice to decipher some passenger-list garbles. The letters of my own name have assumed some twenty different permutations, but I am most often listed simply as Jane Phurber, a winsome six-foot Ohio matron who affects men's

* Publisher's note: He's fifty-eight if he's a day.

clothes. My wife, whose name is Helen Thurber, turned up on one ship under the alias of H. Muriel. In some mysterious manner, our false names (I was Joseph Thacher on this occasion) followed us ashore when we debarked at Naples. My wife indignantly showed our true passport names to one Italian official who had insisted we were one J. Thacher and one H. Muriel. He saw his mistake.

"I am all of regret, *signorina*," he said, in excellent English, "and expressing sorrows towards you and Signor Muriel."

"Come on, H.," I said, "let's go."

"O.K., Joe," she said, and we got out of there.

You will most likely have been at sea a week before you get around to reading the literature you picked up at your travel agency, or at the offices of the steamship line itself. This company gets out a pamphlet entitled *General Information*, and you should have read it before you got on the ship. It lists a number of things that should not be carried in a passenger's luggage: "Dangerous articles, such as fireworks, matches, gunpowder, inflammable liquids, cartridges, inflammable motion-picture films." If you have a supply of skyrockets and Roman candles, it would be wise to dump them overboard some night when nobody is watching you. Skyrockets shot from decks accidentally or out of a misguided burst of patriotic spirit, are certain to be construed as signals of distress by other vessels, and

The Pleasure Cruise, and How to Survive It

this would vex the commander of your ship, to say the least. So leave your fireworks at home, in a safe, locked place, where the children can't get at them. I don't know why you keep fireworks in your house, anyway, but, of course, that is none of my business.

If you have gone on a cruise to relax, and you don't want to romp, run, race or wrassle, stay away from the sports director, a big, energetic blond young man carrying a medicine ball. The female of this species, the sports directress, is active, alert, athletic, aggressive and capable of throwing your wife, or you, over her shoulder with her left hand. If you are not in training and under twenty-eight, don't monkey around with these two. They will run you ragged. They love squatting exercises, chinning themselves, holding their breath, standing on their hands, and touching the deck two thousand times with their finger tips, without bending their knees. Don't try to keep up with them. Refuse their challenges, ignore their taunts. You can't beat them at anything from squatting to ping-pong, unless you are young Mathias, the decathlon champion, and you probably aren't. The sports directors are supposed to organize group recreational activities. This is both a fact and a warning.

Speaking of ping-pong, I once entered a table-tennis tournament aboard the *S.S. President Garfield*, on a trip from New York through the Canal to Los

Angeles. The sports director was determined to get me into the table-tennis tournament, probably because he wanted to see me humiliated in the finals. And he did. I lost two straight games to a pretty, attractive young lady, twenty years * my junior. The table was too short, the net was too high, the rackets were warped, the ship rocked, a small boy among the spectators began riding me and I got something in my eye. I explained to my opponent after the match that, on land and under fair and reasonable conditions, I could have pinned her ears back, the best day she ever saw. She was honest enough to admit this. A very pleasant girl, and the luckiest woman I have ever met on sea or land.

The night before a ship makes home port at the end of a cruise, there is usually a ship's concert, or program of entertainment, in which the Courtney sisters and other gifted passengers are invited to take part. If you are a singer, violinist, bird caller, soft-shoe dancer, whistler, mimic, monologist, contortionist, juggler, hypnotist, ventriloquist, swami, *diseuse* or zither player, you are likely to be asked to join in the fun and do your act. You may refuse, of course, and you should, if you plan to recite all of *Evangeline* or *Hiawatha*. Your fellow passengers will resent any act that lasts longer than five minutes. Once, coming back from the West Indies on the *Conte Grande*, I declined

* Publisher's note: Twenty-two years.

to appear on the concert program, and then suddenly, during a lull at midnight, I grabbed up a lighted megaphone and sang *Who?* and *Bye, Bye, Blackbird* with the orchestra. Well, not *with* it, exactly, since in *Blackbird*, I was singing "*Oh, the hard-luck stories they all hand me*" while the orchestra was playing *No one here can love or understand me*, but we were tied at the finish, I am happy to say. The survivors of that concert will doubtless remember my act, but they will not care to dwell on it any more than I do.

Since my performance that midnight, and possibly because of it, some of the more cautious cruise ships have eliminated passenger participation and turned the program of the final night over to professionals. The last cruise I was on, a few months ago, had no place for amateurs on the Big Night. The entertainment department of WOR provided a soprano, a baritone (to replace me), a prestidigitator, a couple of "dance stylists," an accordionist and several other instrumentalists. Talented passengers who had counted on imitating Tallulah Bankhead or playing Canadian Capers on a makeshift xylophone composed of White Rock bottles were somewhat mollified when they were given funny hats to wear, horns to blow, bells to ring, and rattles to rattle at the Gala Farewell Dinner that preceded the Gala Farewell Revue. In charge of these Galas, and such affairs as the Fancy Headdress Ball and other intellectual goings on, are the cruise

273

director and the cruise directress (not to be confused with the sports director and the sports directress). When, on my recent cruise, I returned to my stateroom after the Gala Farewell Revue, I found a cheerful note from the cruise director. It read: "Rise up in the morning with the will that—smooth or rough—you'll grin!" I decided against this. You never know how a customs man may interpret a grin, especially a fixed grin.

Customs inspection is seldom as trying as you think it's going to be, unless you have a shoeful of diamonds or a trunk full of liqueurs. Just take your place under your proper letter (*Q* for Smith, *E* for Perkins, *P* for Thurber, and so forth) and see that you have assembled all your baggage. You will usually find that your typewriter case is missing and that you have a large gray suitcase that doesn't belong to you. The person who owns the gray suitcase may have your typewriter, and he may not. Don't get excited and rush around accusing people of stealing your Corona, just relax. You have all day, you know, and if you went to bed instead of to the bar after the Gala Revue, you will find yourself taking this ancient formality in your stride. It is important not to get mad at your inspector because he wants to go through your effects. That is his job. A Virginian I know, a man impatient of red tape and fiddle-faddle, as he describes all activities of the United States Government, once addressed a group of three customs inspectors as follows: "Gentlemen, you are clearly insane." He was the last man off the dock that day.

No travel hints would be complete without some word of caution about shipboard romances, engagements and marriages. The girl or young man you fell in love with on the ship when it was in Southern waters and the orchestra was playing "Night and Day" is going to be subjected to a cruel and rigorous test standing there by a gloomy pile of baggage in a bleak and chilly ship shed. If the swan suddenly becomes a goose, or the knight a clodhopper, it is what is known as "undergoing a land change." If you were married aboard ship, and the bride, or bridegroom, now appeals to you about as much as a piece of cold whole-wheat toast, you are in a rather serious jam. In America you cannot have a marriage annulled on the ground that it was contracted while you were under the influence of the Gulf Stream and Cole Porter. If you are a man, I suggest that you treat your inamorata with gallantry tempered by caution during the voyage out and back, and refrain from proposing until you have caught her on the dock. If she is going to be met by her mother and father, her Aunt Louise and her Uncle Bert, you will want to get a look at them first too. During the cruise try to engage the girl of your dreams in discussions of books or politics if you find yourself with her on the promenade deck in the

275

moonlight, while the band is playing "I Told Every Little Star." It won't work, but try it. All this, I suppose, is really no more concern of mine than why you keep fireworks in the house, so I will not pursue it further.

I hope that the foregoing helpful hints for a happy holiday will make your future sea voyages a little easier and merrier and safer. You need not, to be sure, take my advice or follow my example, in every situation and contretemps I have described hereinabove. If you want to put the shoe back on the sick lady's foot, or just leave it where you found it, feel free to do so. The reason I put the shoe on the table with the handbag was—but we have been all through that. I am beginning to repeat myself. Bon Voyage!